Seahenge:

Charlie Watson

AN **ARCHAEOLOGICAL** Conundrum

ENGLISH HERITAGE

Published by English Heritage, Kemble Drive, Swindon SN2 2GZ

www.english-heritage.org.uk

English Heritage is the Government's statutory adviser on all aspects of the historic environment.

© English Heritage 2005

Printing 10 9 8 7 6 5 4 3 2 1

Images (except as otherwise shown) © English Heritage

First published 2005

ISBN 1 85074 896 9

Product Code 50887

British Library Cataloguing in Publication data
A CIP catalogue record for this book is available from the British Library.

The National Monuments Record is the public archive of English Heritage. For more information, contact NMR Enquiry and Research Services, National Monuments Record Centre, Kemble Drive, Swindon SN2 2GZ; telephone (01793) 414600.

Edited and brought to publication by David M Jones, Publishing, English Heritage, Kemble Drive, Swindon SN2 2GZ.
Indexed by the author
Page layout by Patricia Briggs
Picture research by Diana Phillips

Printed in the UK by The Bath Press, Bath.

Opposite: *The mysterious timber circle at Holme-next-the-Sea, slowly revealed by the shifting sands in 1998.*

Overleaf: *A relic of the Bronze Age – the timber circle was built on a saltmarsh, spent millennia beneath the waves, and re-emerged on a beach.*

Pages x–xi: *At low tide, the eroding peat scarps, the part-exposed timber circle and the hulking central tree stump present a beautiful yet eerie scene.*

Seahenge:
Charlie Watson

AN **ARCHAEOLOGICAL** Conundrum

foreword by **Francis Pryor**

CONTENTS

'I was staggered when I first saw it. I had goose pimples. It really was like stepping back 4,000 years. It's unique. It is of enormous international importance.'

Francis Pryor

'There are an awful lot of people out there who don't care about the past, and these people, I think, are a serious worry. Because if you don't care about the past, you don't care about humanity, and that's what makes us civilised.'

Francis Pryor

FOREWORD

Every so often an archaeological find captures the public imagination. The timber circle on the beach at Holme-next-the-Sea was just such a discovery. It was first recognised by a local enthusiast, John Lorimer, in the spring of 1998. To his credit John promptly reported it to the authorities. Soon the press got hold of the story and dubbed the circle 'Seahenge'. In some respects that name is unfortunate as the site is neither a 'henge', as archaeologists define the word, nor was it built on the seashore, but rather in a backswamp behind coastal dunes. Still, it's memorable – and has stuck.

Studies of Holme beach had shown that 'Seahenge' was under imminent threat of destruction by the sea, and the brave decision to excavate and remove the timbers from harm's way was taken by Dr Geoffrey Wainwright, then Chief Archaeologist at English Heritage. This decision was contested vigorously by Pagans, Druids, aesthetes and others who wanted the circle to remain in place, even though that would inevitably result in its destruction by the sea.

A team from Norfolk County Council Archaeological Service, under Mark Brennand's resolute leadership, were contracted to do the work. Their work was to prove both difficult and sometimes dangerous. As they excavated, they were struck by the fact that the vast majority of the many visitors to the dig were strongly in favour of what they were doing. Both excavators and visitors alike were convinced that the site must be rescued for posterity, and I am glad to report that its final resting place will be where it belongs, in the town of King's Lynn.

There has been one unexpected development. The wealth of information revealed by the study of the timbers, and the manner of their erection in the year 2049 BC, has told us more about prehistoric ritual and religion than any other single site in the history of British Bronze Age archaeology. These extraordinary revelations are constantly being discussed by archaeologists and others interested in the past. So my response to those who were prepared to see 'Seahenge' drown, is that it has now acquired a vigorous 'after life' in the realms of the living. May that new life continue to thrive.

Francis Pryor MBE
President of the Council for British Archaeology

ILLUSTRATION CREDITS

Figures are reproduced by kind permission as follows:

All photographs are copyright of English Heritage, unless otherwise stated.

Archaeoptics 19, 60, 69
John Byford 8(br),23(b)
Colchester Museum 77
Devizes Museum 49(l)
Eastern Daily Press 2, 3, 39, 39, 42, 47, 51, 54(both), 55, 57, 80, 85
Empics 47(t)
Pat Fisher 47(b)
Heritage Images 6(tr), 8(tr)
Gary Hibberd 10(all), 30
Holt Studios 5(t&br) 46, 73(t)
The Independent 27
Graham Johnston 52(b)
King's Lynn Museum 84
Mary Rose Trust 83(r), 83(l)/Photo Pete Langdown

National Museum Denmark 22
Natural History Museum, London 73
Nolfolk Heritage Centre 5(bl)
© Norfolk Museums & Archaeology Service and photo by Mark Brennand 17, 43(t), 52(t), 79; Jason Dawson 3(t), 33(both), 35, 38, 40(both), 41, 59, 66(b); P M Goodchild & Son 81; Fran Green 18(both), 20, 64(b), 66(t); Edwin Rose 12
Mike Page 28–29, 89
Mike Pitts 34, 86
The Prehistoric Society 14, 18, 25, 64, 61, 67
Francis Pryor 1, 3(b), 13 ,23(t), 58(t&b), 63, 72, 3, 24, 58
Salisbury Museum 49(r)

Science Photo Library 69
Penny Waterhouse ,27, 31(b), 50
Sue White 6(l), 48

Applications for reproduction of images should be made to the National Monuments Record. English Heritage has endeavoured to ensure that full permission has been sought and given for all material used in this publication. Every effort has been made to trace the copyright holders and we apologise in advance for any unintentional omissions, which we would be pleased to correct in any subsequent edition of this book.

ACKNOWLEDGEMENTS

The story of the discovery, excavation and analysis of the timber circle at Holme-next-the-Sea is a fascinating one, but one whose details were hidden away in any number of file boxes, newspaper archives, previous publications and, of course, the memories, diaries and desk drawers of those involved. Pulling the information together could have been a daunting task.

Happily, though, it wasn't. In almost every case, people went out of their way to offer documents, photographs, contacts, interpretations, ideas, mugs of tea and, most valuable of all, their time.

At English Heritage, Val Horsler and Kath Buxton set the project running, and Judith Dobie produced four beautiful and imaginative illustrations. David Jones was a patient and sympathetic editor, who paid great attention to the detail of the text and shepherded the project to completion.

At the Norfolk Archaeological Unit, Andy Shelley recruited me to the team and Jayne Bown oversaw the project, while David Adams and Fran Green generously shared their recollections of life in the trenches. At Norfolk Landscape Archaeology in Gressenhall, Edwin Rose recalled his early visits to the beach, and Jan Allen trawled the photographic archive. Norfolk's county archaeologist, Brian Ayers, remembered the tense meetings between the archaeologists and the protesters, and explained the finer points of the relationship between the historic environment, archaeology and the public's perception of archaeology.

In north-west Norfolk, Robin Hanley, Gary Hibberd, John Lorimer and Michael Meakin explained events from the points of view of the area museums officer, the nature reserve warden, the discoverer of the timber circle and the landowner respectively. Across the border in Lincolnshire, Francis Pryor and Maisie Taylor provided photographs of the excavation, plus insight into the Time Team reconstruction and the mysteries of ancient timber.

Later in the process, Diana Phillips did a marvellous job of researching pictures and illustrations, and designer Patricia Briggs turned raw words and pictures into a coherent and stylish whole.

And finally Mark Brennand, the site director at Holme-next-the-Sea in 1999, read the book in draft form, chapter by chapter, correcting mistakes of fact and emphasis and making many valuable suggestions.

My sincere thanks to them all.

Charlie Watson

1 Discovery

John Lorimer's walk on the beach

John Lorimer is a regular visitor to the beaches of north-west Norfolk. He is a special-needs worker who takes care of children and young people with learning and other disabilities, and a trip to the beach can be a very positive and enjoyable activity. He is also an enthusiastic beachcomber and amateur archaeologist who loves the ever-changing coastal environment. But on a particular day in early spring, 1998, it was neither his youngsters nor the latest flotsam and jetsam left by the tide that brought John to the beach at Holme-next-the-Sea. The plan that day was to catch shrimps.

John and his brother-in-law Gary had come to Holme to try out a new shrimping net Gary had made. As they climbed the dunes at the back of the beach, though, they realised the tide was not yet far enough out – only when the sea had retreated beyond the exposed peat beds would they be able to pull the new net through the water. Instead, they decided to spend an hour or so crabbing.

The dunes at Holme beach are the natural sea

Eroding peat beds on Holme beach in 1998.

defences of the Holme Dunes National Nature Reserve. For the most part, they are like the dunes elsewhere along the north Norfolk coast, dominated by marram grass and some sea holly, and home to birds such as the meadow pipit and skylark. At the point where John and Gary had walked over them, however, the Holme Dunes ran in front of a small wood of Corsican pines, probably planted during the late 19th century as part of a series of measures to encourage the build-up of sand. Although the native Scots pine thrives in many coastal locations, the Corsican pine is a more robust species and is better suited to the harsh weather that sometimes sweeps across The Wash and on to the low-lying north Norfolk shore.

Today, though, the sun was shining as John and Gary made their way down to the shallow water at the edge of the peat beds. The peat was the remains of coastal woodland that was drowned between 4,000 and 4,500 years ago, and the pools and crevices among the peat beds made perfect homes and hide-outs for the tasty, elusive crabs. But before the crab-hunt was properly under way, John spotted something else, something green and metallic lying in the silty mud. He picked it up and looked at it. It was not iron, for sure – much more likely to be brass, a fitting from a wrecked ship perhaps. Or might it, just possibly, be something more ancient?

Gary thought not. To him, the lump of metal John was turning over in his hands was almost certainly a piece of scrap from a shipwreck. Not from just any shipwreck, but most probably from the *Vicuna*, whose remaining timbers were beginning to emerge from the waves 150m (c 500 ft) away. The *Vicuna* was a freighter that had been carrying a cargo of Norwegian ice to King's Lynn in 1883. Forced to shelter in the Humber estuary from a violent storm, she had broken her moorings and been driven south, finally going aground near Brancaster, several miles east of Holme-next-the-Sea, on March 7, 1883. Since then, storms and tides had shifted the wreck along the Norfolk coastline several times, and the battered remains had arrived at Holme, not far above the low-water mark, after a surge tide in 1985.

The *Vicuna* explanation seemed a reasonable one, but John put the piece of metal in his pocket none the less. For now, though, there was a new shrimping net to test, and the tide was far enough out to use it. The two friends waded out into the shallow water and got to work.

During the next few weeks, John returned to Holme beach several times, looking for crabs and shrimp, but revisiting, too, the spot where he had found the mysterious piece of metal. It was on one of these trips that he first noticed a large tree stump, with two worn-down branches. Although the stump was the same colour as the peat nearby – and the beach was the site of a drowned forest, after all – the lone tree-stump looked somehow out of place. No others stood proud of the surface like this one and, in any case, why would only one tree survive? And why, when John reached down into the silt beside the stump, could he feel no roots fanning out, but only the smooth side of the trunk?

The other puzzle was the strange piece of metal on John's mantelpiece in the village of North Creake. With every day that passed, he felt more and more certain that it had not come from the *Vicuna*. Although ships of the Victorian era had lots of brass fittings, this odd-shaped lump of metal did not look like a section of porthole rim or anything else John could imagine. One end of it looked like a simple, crescent-shaped axe head, but it was not big enough or well enough finished to be a ship's fire-fighting axe and surely would not be made of brass if it were. Instead, it still bore hammer marks and a 'casting line' that showed where the two halves of the mould had met when the molten metal was cast.

John was not convinced that it was brass, either. Perhaps it was bronze. And if it was, then maybe, just maybe, it was a Bronze Age axe head.

John's next move was to call a friend of his in Fakenham who was an enthusiastic metal-detectorist. He might have come across something like this before, John thought, and even if he had not, John could consult his friend's many metal-detecting magazines for other clues and ideas.

The battered remains of the Vicuna, wrecked near Brancaster in 1883 and a curiosity on Holme beach since 1985.

The magazine strategy turned out to be a good one. Among features on coins, belt buckles and umpteen other metal objects that metal-detectorists often come across, John found one on Bronze Age metalworking. Better still, it was accompanied by a picture of a 3,000-year-old bronze axe head. It was not exactly the same as his, but it was close enough. What he had found, he now felt sure, was an ancient axe head. What John wanted to know now, however, was just how ancient it was and what it was doing on the beach at Holme. Back at home, he picked up the phone and called the Castle Museum at Norwich.

The archaeologists at Castle Museum kept the axe head for almost a month. It did indeed date from the Bronze Age – about 1200 BC – they confirmed, and was very similar to another Bronze Age axe head that had been discovered on Holme beach and brought to them for analysis at about the same time. Although John's axe head was not so well preserved, and was thus harder to identify, their opinion was that it had probably been made in Ireland.

The Bronze Age axe head found by John Lorimer during a trip to the beach to try out a new shrimping net.

An early picture of the timber circle, with sand dunes and dune defences in the background.

While the experts had been examining the axe head, John had made several more trips to Holme beach. He found no further bronze artefacts, but instead was captivated by the gradual change in the appearance of the lone tree stump. It was situated in a bare patch of silty mud, where the peat bed had eroded away, and the scouring action of the waves was exposing a little more of it each time John visited. Then one day he noticed another, smaller stump a few feet away. The next day the

waves had exposed another and, over the course of several days, an entire ring of stumps became clearly visible around the original, and much bigger, central tree. There was no mistaking it. But … a *circle* of stumps? Surely that could not be a natural remnant of the ancient drowned forest. It had to be something man-made – perhaps made by the same people who had used the small bronze axe. John picked up the phone to call the Castle Museum archaeologists again.

Norfolk's evolving landscape

The Norfolk landscape has changed enormously over time. Today it is dominated by productive agricultural land, drained in low-lying areas by systems of dykes and windpumps, and graced still by many tall windmills, symbols of the energy and efficiency of Norfolk farmers during recent centuries. But this contemporary picture is very different from the one that greeted the first humans – *Homo erectus* rather than *Homo sapiens* – to explore the area, about 400,000 BC.

The land that would later become Norfolk was then between ice ages, which covered it for tens of

(Above) The modern face of Norfolk: a productive agricultural landscape very different from the mixed woodland and heaths that were home to Mesolithic hunter-gatherers.

(Below left) Agriculture then: for millennia, farming was labour-intensive and dependent on working animals.

(Below) Agriculture now: mechanisation and electronic technology have revolutionised farming though the past century.

5

(Left) A Mesolithic hunter and his tools: a barbed antler point and a flint-tipped spear.

Daggers drawn: (left to right) modern copy of a hafted flint dagger of Beaker type; flint dagger of Beaker type (c 2000–1600 BC); bone dagger copying a hafted copper dagger (c 1800–1600 BC); copper dagger in modern wooden haft (c 2000–1800 BC).

thousands of years in thick ice sheets – the Anglian ice age lasted from 500,000 to 400,000 years ago, and the Wolstonian from 200,000 to 130,000 years ago. Sea levels were much lower, too, so much of the North Sea was dry land, as was the English Channel, making Britain part of the continental landmass for long periods. Pollen analysis reveals that Norfolk was an area of mixed pine and birch woodland for much of the 'interglacial' periods, and discoveries of flint tools – axes, scrapers and knives – across the county suggest a nomadic lifestyle of hunting, gathering and camping along river valleys and lake shores. Likely food sources included beaver, deer, elephant, horse, pig and rhinoceros, as well as roots, fruits and leaves. The return of the ice about 115,000 years ago, however, forced these early human inhabitants to retreat southward.

During this most recent ice age (the Devensian) the ice sheet did not reach as far south as Norfolk, but the landscape was a frozen tundra. When the ice finally retreated, about 10,000 BC, a new transformation of the landscape began. The moving ice sheets, particularly of the Wolstonian Period, had transported and deposited vast quantities of the sands, gravels, loams and heavy boulder clays that characterise Norfolk today. Now plants and trees were able to colonise the newly thawed ground, then open woodlands of birch, pine and willow. These were followed by species such as oak, elm, lime and hazel as the climate warmed from about 8500 BC. Until this point, the sea level was some 60m (c 197ft) lower than it is today, which allowed hunters to roam far to the north and east of today's Norfolk coastline. Dramatic evidence of this appeared in 1931, when a trawler operating 25 miles (c 40km) north-east of Cromer dredged up a barbed antler point. Identified as a fish spear, the antler point has been radiocarbon-dated to about 9800 BC.

As the climate became milder, although still colder than today, new groups of people continued to arrive in eastern England from the continent. These Mesolithic peoples roamed across Norfolk, catching fish, hunting birds and forest animals, and gathering plant foods. Archaeological finds show that these people worked flint to produce blades, scrapers, tips for arrows and spears, and a distinctive axe known as a 'tranchet' axe, sharpened by striking a transverse blow across the cutting edge. One particularly rich site, on Kelling Heath, has yielded hundreds of flint artefacts. From here, high on the Cromer Ridge, the hunters would have had a panoramic view over the wide plain that today is covered by the North Sea,

enabling them to spot their prey with ease.

As temperatures slowly rose, however, so did the sea level. The land bridge to the continent had disappeared by about 6500 BC, and the Fens were becoming inundated. These changes, together with the replacement of relatively open coniferous woodland by much denser deciduous forest, forced these early East Anglians to adapt their lifestyles.

On the continent, a new way of life was evolving, which included settled communities, domesticated animals and the production of arable crops. Although no hard evidence of Mesolithic farming has been found in Norfolk, it is likely that the tranchet axe was used to clear land, even if only for seasonal camps and pathways, and that Mesolithic people gradually increased the proportion of cultivated food and domesticated animals in their diet.

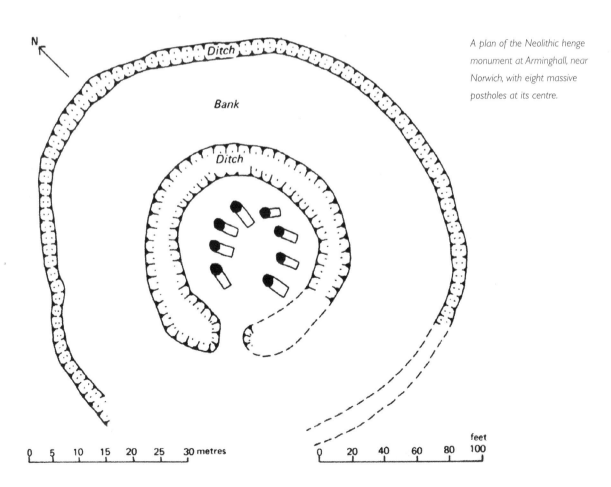

A plan of the Neolithic henge monument at Arminghall, near Norwich, with eight massive postholes at its centre.

Late Neolithic/Early Bronze Age ceramic beaker, European, c 4000 BC.

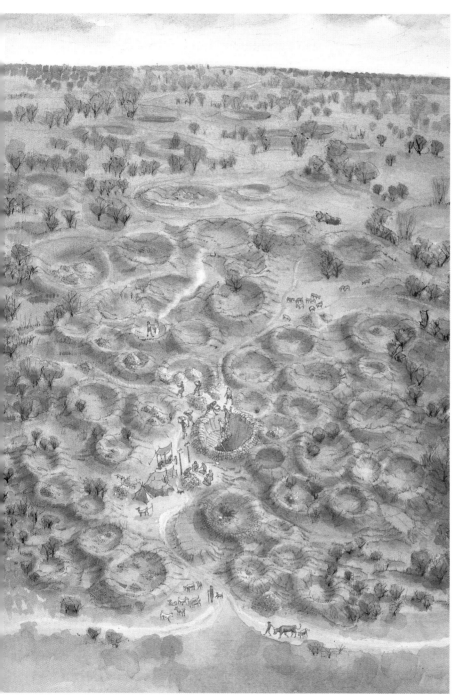

At the Neolithic flint mines at Grimes Graves in south-west Norfolk, more than 360 shafts (each up to 40 ft deep; c 12 m) are still visible as hollows on the surface.

A Bronze Age spearhead, c 800–1300 BC, from Flag Fen in Cambridgeshire

By 4000 BC, though, early farmers were hard at work in Norfolk. As well as learning how to work the land, these later Neolithic people had developed (or imported) other techniques: they made simple pottery from clay, sharpened and polished flint axes by grinding, and used flint-bladed sickles to harvest arable crops and querns to grind grain. For example excavations at Redgate Hill, Hunstanton, six miles (c 9.7 km) from Holme-next-the-Sea, have produced Neolithic plant remains including emmer (a primitive wheat), barley and hazelnuts, and animal bones such as sheep and goat from the Earlier Neolithic period and pigs, cattle, dear, goat, wildcat and dolphin from the Later Neolithic, together with shells of cockles, mussels and oysters.

Other signs of technological and social change in this period are visible in the landscape, although sometimes only from aerial photographs. Across Britain, Neolithic people were building long barrow burial mounds, of which four are still visible in Norfolk, at Broome Heath, Felthorpe, Harpley and West Rudham. Cropmarks elsewhere in the county suggest that many other long barrows might have been destroyed by ploughing.

At Arminghall, two miles from Norwich, an even more dramatic structure was built: a 'henge monument' consisting of a circular bank 50 ft (c 15.25 m) wide and with a diameter of 260 ft (c 79.25 m), with inner and outer ditches and, at its heart, a horseshoe of eight massive postholes. Each posthole originally contained a timber up to 3 ft (c 1 m) in diameter, sunk 7½ ft (c 2.3 m) into the ground – radiocarbon tests date the timbers to between 3500 BC and 2700 BC.

The exact purpose of the timbers is not clear. They might have supported a roof and walls, or each one could have been a free-standing totem. Whichever it was, the construction of the Arminghall monument was an impressive demonstration of the technical and organisational abilities of Norfolk's Neolithic inhabitants.

Even more eye-opening, perhaps, are the Neolithic flint mines at Grimes Graves, near Weeting in south-west Norfolk. Begun in the Later Neolithic period, the mines were actively exploited well into the Bronze Age. More than 500 shafts up to 40 ft (c 12 m) deep have been found, of which 360 are still visible as hollows, plus 1,600 shallow, opencast pits. Estimates of the number of implements made from the high-grade black flint mined at Grimes Graves run into the millions, a substantial number of which found their way to other locations in the British Isles, just as tools made from stone found in south-west and north-west England were transported to Norfolk.

The first metal artefacts probably arrived in Norfolk some time after 2500 BC. Made of bronze, a copper–tin alloy, these objects have been found throughout the county, rivalled in number and quality by only a few other areas in Britain. These finds show that this was a time not only of technological innovation, but also of increasing wealth, land clearance and, almost certainly, population. From about this time, too, Earlier Bronze Age people began to use 'beaker' pottery (a fine, decorated earthenware also found in the Low Countries and northern Germany) and to construct characteristic round burial mounds in large numbers. More than 600 'round barrows' have been recorded in Norfolk, with hundreds more revealed by aerial photography as ploughed-out 'ring-ditches'.

While Bronze Age burial sites are well documented in the county, settlement sites are much harder to find. In part, this is due to the destructive effects of urban growth and intensive agriculture, but it is also likely that Bronze Age dwellings were short-lived and thus left few traces. Some archaeologists even argue that there were no permanent dwellings. There is no doubt, however, that Bronze Age people were present and active in north-west Norfolk. Bronze Age hoards – collections of deliberately buried ornaments and tools – have been found locally; there is strong evidence of a Later Neolithic/Bronze Age settlement at Redgate Hill in Hunstanton; and there are round barrows throughout the area. A group of four ring-ditches has been identified just 2.5km south-east of the site of John Lorimer's discovery, for example, and fragments of beaker pottery have been found a little farther south-east again. As elsewhere in Britain, Bronze Age people in north-west Norfolk were changing the landscape, developing new farming techniques and gradually accumulating wealth. It was a busy time.

Wildlife in the Holme Dunes reserve: grey plover (top, left), natterjack toad (top, right), knots (centre) and little terns (bottom).

Holme Dunes National Nature Reserve

While human activity in north-west Norfolk was on the increase 4,000 years ago, today the area immediately surrounding the site of John Lorimer's discovery is the Holme Dunes National Nature Reserve, managed by the Norfolk Wildlife Trust. Situated at the point on the north Norfolk coast where the Wash meets the North Sea, the 281 ha (629 acre) reserve includes a rich mix of coastal habitats, from saltmarsh and sand dunes to sand and shingle bars, intertidal sands and mudflats, freshwater and brackish pools, reedbed and grazing marsh. The River Hun flows peacefully through the reserve from west to east.

Many bird and other species make the Holme Dunes reserve their seasonal home. During summer, for example, meadow pipits, skylarks, linnets, lesser whitethroats and grasshopper warblers nest in the dunes; redshanks breed on the saltmarsh; little terns, ringed plovers and oystercatchers find nesting sites on the shingle ridges and foredunes; and lapwing, snipe and avocets inhabit the grazing marshes. In winter, the visitors include Brent geese, long-tailed ducks, common scoters, golden plovers, sanderlings and – in internationally important numbers – grey plovers, knots and bar-tailed godwits. Bitterns are also seen occasionally in spring and autumn. Non-bird wildlife on the reserve includes pipistrelle and noctule bats, stoats, rabbits, brown hares and a strong population of natterjack toads, introduced in 1981. Butterfly species include grayling, brown argus and, rarely, the grizzled skipper, and some 350 species of moth have been recorded.

The significance of this diverse range of habitats and wildlife is clear from the number of special designations the Holme Dunes reserve has received. It has been made a Special Area of Conservation (SAC) and a Special Protection Area (SPA) by the European Union, a National Nature Reserve (NNR) and a Site of Special Scientific Interest (SSSI) by the UK government, and a 'Ramsar' (a site of international importance for wetland habitats and birds) under an international convention signed in Ramsar, Iran.

The Three Age System

For convenience in describing developments in culture and technology, as well as the movement of people, the past is divided into periods. The 'historical period' covers that part of the past for which there are written records, and the 'prehistoric period' is the earlier time for which there are no written records. In Britain, the beginning of the historic period is accepted as AD 43, the year of the Roman invasion.

In turn, prehistory has conventionally been subdivided into three ages: the Stone Age, the Bronze Age and the Iron Age (see time chart). These divisions were proposed in 1819 by Danish archaeologist Christian Jurgensen Thomsen, who was classifying artefacts in the new National Museum in Copenhagen. His theory was that early technologies had developed in chronological stages, which could be described in terms of the predominant material used to make tools and weapons: first stone, then bronze and, later, iron.

Thomsen's central idea has been proved essentially correct, although it is less useful in describing the development of technology in parts of the world outside Europe, the Middle East and Egypt. Over time, it has also been refined, first by the subdivision of the Stone Age into the Palaeolithic, Mesolithic and Neolithic Ages, and subsequently by the subdivision of the Neolithic, Bronze and Iron Ages into early, middle and late periods. Most recently, the subdivisions of the Neolithic, Bronze and Iron Ages have been redefined as 'earlier' and 'later' (not shown on the time chart).

Table of dates and periods (adapted from Seahenge: A Quest for Life and Death in Bronze Age Britain, *by Francis Pryor).*

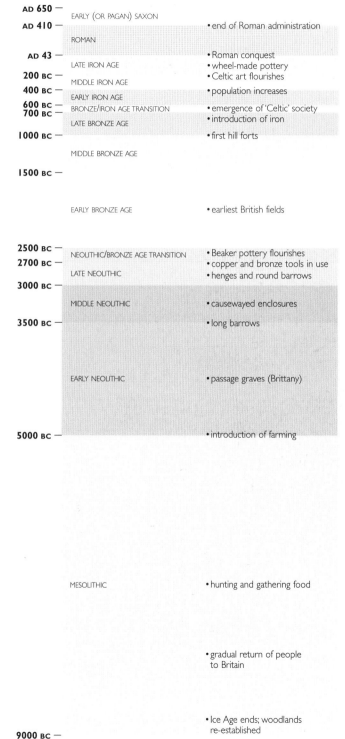

AD 650 —	EARLY (OR PAGAN) SAXON	
AD 410 —		• end of Roman administration
	ROMAN	
AD 43 —		• Roman conquest
	LATE IRON AGE	• wheel-made pottery
200 BC —		• Celtic art flourishes
400 BC —	MIDDLE IRON AGE	
	EARLY IRON AGE	• population increases
600 BC —	BRONZE/IRON AGE TRANSITION	• emergence of 'Celtic' society
700 BC —		• introduction of iron
	LATE BRONZE AGE	• first hill forts
1000 BC —		
	MIDDLE BRONZE AGE	
1500 BC —		
	EARLY BRONZE AGE	• earliest British fields
2500 BC —	NEOLITHIC/BRONZE AGE TRANSITION	• Beaker pottery flourishes
2700 BC —		• copper and bronze tools in use
	LATE NEOLITHIC	• henges and round barrows
3000 BC —		
	MIDDLE NEOLITHIC	• causewayed enclosures
3500 BC —		• long barrows
	EARLY NEOLITHIC	• passage graves (Brittany)
5000 BC —		• introduction of farming
	MESOLITHIC	• hunting and gathering food
		• gradual return of people to Britain
9000 BC —		• Ice Age ends; woodlands re-established

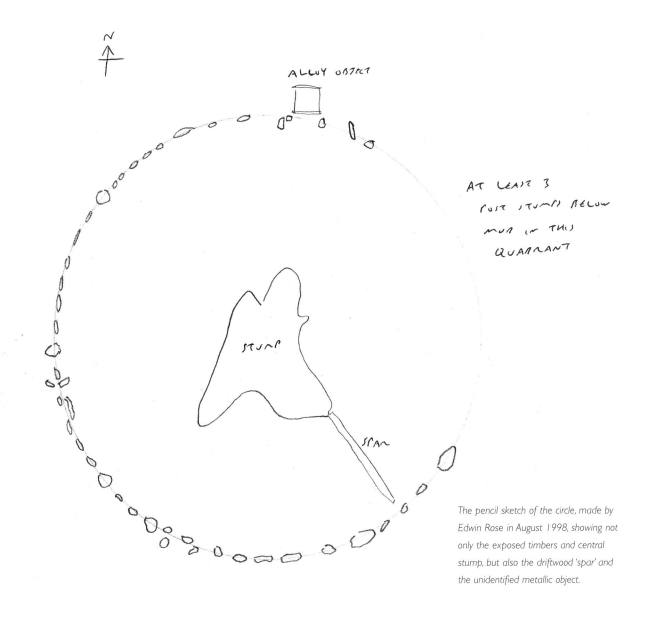

ALLOY OBJECT

N

AT LEAST 3
POST STUMPS BELOW
MUD IN THIS
QUADRANT

STUMP

SPAR

The pencil sketch of the circle, made by Edwin Rose in August 1998, showing not only the exposed timbers and central stump, but also the driftwood 'spar' and the unidentified metallic object.

Maintaining this complex and fragile ecosystem, however, is not easy. For example, sand dunes and saltmarshes are naturally dynamic systems, but for some years the scouring action of the sea has been lowering the level of the beach on the reserve (although sand is accreting elsewhere along the north-east Norfolk coast), causing the base of the dunes to be undercut by strong waves. Any breach of the main dune system would seriously affect the reserve's fresh water and brackish water habitats. Changing animal

populations make a difference, too: fox numbers have grown since the 1980s, presenting a serious threat to ground-nesting birds. One of the biggest dangers, though, is people. A long-distance coast path runs east–west through the dunes, intersecting a number of smaller paths; in some areas, plants are trampled and, as walkers seek access to the beach, gullies that are created in the dunes are swiftly exploited by the wind. In addition, 'rights of common' are held by many residents of Holme-next-the-Sea and Thornham,

entitling them to use the intertidal, dune and saltmarsh areas for activities such as wildfowling and the gathering of samphire, shellfish, seaweed, sea lavender, soil and bait. So, although the Holme Dunes reserve welcomes careful visitors, it really does not want too many.

The view westward along Holme beach, showing the rapidly eroding layer of peat that had protected the timber circle for thousands of years.

A fish trap or something more interesting?

John Lorimer's report of a circle of timber posts near the site of his axe-head find was passed on to Edwin Rose, then Norfolk Landscape Archaeology's Development Control Officer, based at the Gressenhall Museum of Rural Life. 'Anything that needed looking at came to me,' says Rose, 'so I went along to the reserve at Holme on 12 August and met John and his wife and children. He took us across the beach to the circle, and at first I thought it was probably one of the Saxon fish traps that are always turning up.' John Lorimer remembers being frustrated that Rose was interested in other objects on the

beach, such as the remains of the *Vicuna*, and did not offer immediate confirmation that the circle of posts was something to do with his Bronze Age axe head.

That was not the end of the story, however. By chance, Edwin Rose had left his tape measure in his car, so he made a pencil sketch of the circle and briefly surveyed the peat beds, the beach and the wreck of the *Vicuna* near by. 'Later on,' he recalls, 'I went back to my car to fetch the tape measure, and then came back to the circle. By now I was alone and the tide was coming in fast, so I took the measurements I needed, some black-and-white photographs and a small timber sample for radiocarbon dating, and then left for home.'

At Gressenhall the next day, events began to move faster. Rose reported his findings to David Gurney, the

Principal Landscape Archaeologist, and began working on his report. Gurney wasted no time in contacting the English Heritage head office at Savile Row in London. 'A circle of timber posts has been reported to us in the intertidal zone [at Holme-next-the-Sea],' he wrote, 'where a Bronze Age axe has also been found. Edwin visited the site on 12 August (report enclosed). This sounds very significant, and should be accurately located, properly planned and recorded and dated by C14, if possible. Could English Heritage provide any funds for this? If so, I'll ask the NAU [Norfolk Archaeological Unit] to submit a proposal and costings. We may need to act quickly, as there is some risk and we will need a suitably low tide.'

A day later, on 14 August, Edwin Rose wrote a fuller description of the timber circle:

The feature is halfway between the present high and low water marks on what the Ordnance Survey mark as West Sands, though the composition is now mud above firm clay, in which are embedded the 'people sleepers' or trees of the submerged forest. The feature is more oval than circular and forms a pool at low tide, with the tops of the stakes protruding just above water level. 48 posts are visible, with an apparent gap at the north-east quadrant; but probing here indicated that at least three stakes remain broken off below the surface. The posts at the north-west quadrant are regularly spaced, about 50–70 cm [c 19¾in–27½ in] apart, but the remainder almost overlap and in the south-west quadrant there are posts at right angles to the others, forming small boxed areas. The width of the circle was measured as 7.5 m [c 24½ ft] north–south.

Slightly off-centre to the circle is a massive bucranial tree stump, 1.5 m [c 5 ft] across by 1.75 m [c 5¾ ft] long, at a higher level than the surviving posts. A wooden spar about 2 m [c 6½ ft] long runs south-east from this, but this is probably a piece of driftwood swept into the circle, caught under the stump and cemented by encrustation. In a similar way a large rectangular object of alloy, possibly part of an aircraft, has caught against the north side of the circle, and cannon shells were noted nearby, dating from World War II use as a firing range.

The location of the feature was ascertained by a line projected north-west from the pillbox at the centre of site 23518. It is about 100 m [c 328 ft] south-west of the present position of the wreck of the Vicuna.

– Edwin Rose, 14 August 1998

The ball was now in English Heritage's court, and the question was just how important they thought the find might be. Did it rank high enough on their priority list to warrant further investigation?

The answer was not long in coming. First, a few weeks after Edwin Rose's visit, John Lorimer received a letter from the Norfolk Archaeological Unit, telling him that his discovery had aroused great excitement. Then, English Heritage approved a proposal and costing from the Norfolk Archaeological Unit for a trial excavation and radiocarbon dating. Finally, in October, a team of archaeologists arrived to take a closer look at the discovery and to discuss strategy for the trial excavation. The group included Bill Boismier and Mark Brennand of the Norfolk Archaeological Unit, Peter Murphy, an environmental archaeologist for English Heritage, and Maisie Taylor, an expert on prehistoric wood and the co-founder of the Bronze Age centre at Flag Fen in Cambridgeshire. They were guided to the circle of posts, with its strange tree stump centrepiece, by Gary Hibberd, the resident Warden of the Holme Dunes reserve. Within minutes, the archaeologists knew that what they were looking at was no Saxon fish trap or strange natural configuration of tree stumps from the drowned forest. This was something special.

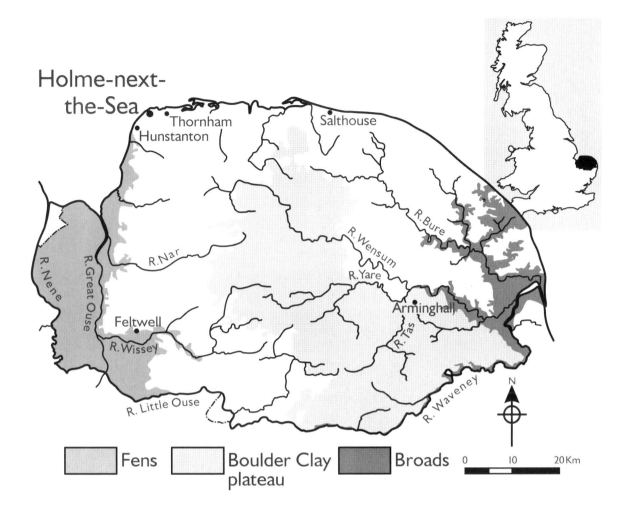

Norfolk, showing the location of Holme-next-the-Sea.

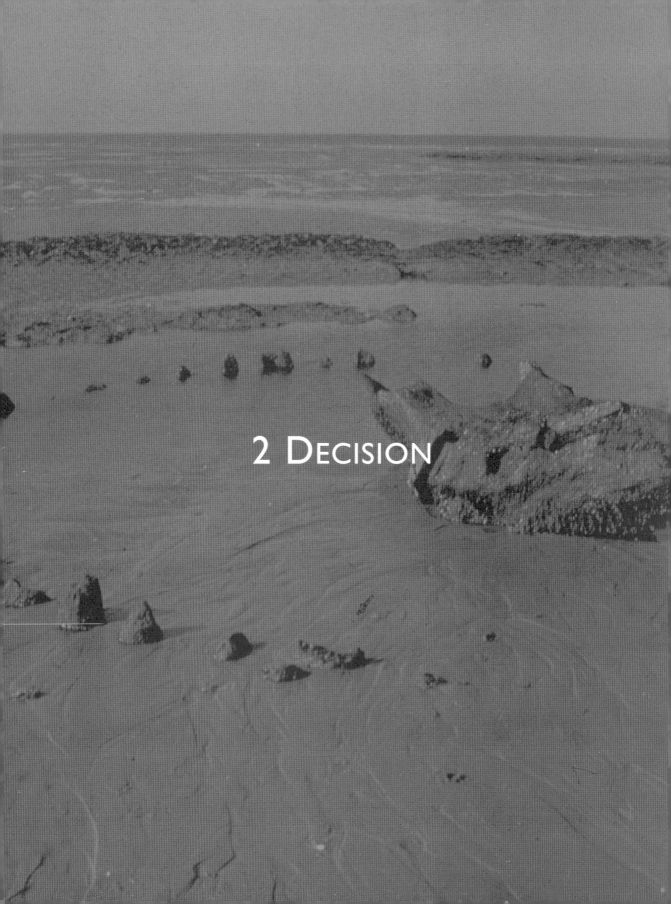

2 DECISION

Evaluating the timber circle

The evaluation of the timber circle began in October 1998. Although no one was yet sure what the mysterious timbers were, it was clear that as more of the circle was exposed by the shifting sands and eroding peat beds, so the timbers were increasingly vulnerable to the scouring action of the waves. There was no time to waste.

The task facing Norfolk Archaeological Unit was not an easy one. The tides limited the team to between one and four on-site working hours per day, and every incoming tide filled the excavation with sand and silt that had to be dug out again the next day before work could progress. Worse still, the speed of the tides was not consistent: sometimes they came in slowly, while at other times the tide had no sooner turned than the advancing waves were halfway up the beach.

The first task faced by site director Mark Brennand's team was to pinpoint the location of the circle – in the absence of any mapped features within the intertidal zone from which to survey, this was done using Global Positioning System (GPS) satellite technology. Next the posts were recorded individually and surveyed, revealing the timber 'circle' to be, in fact, an ellipse (maximum diameter 6.6m or c 21½ft), whose long axis ran north-west to south-east.

For the excavation itself the team dug two trial trenches, one inside the monument, running from the

Examining the circle: before digging a trial trench, Mark Brennand and his team made an accurate survey of the timber circle, revealing it to be an ellipse with an axis running from north-west to south-east. In the background is the wreck of the Vicuna.

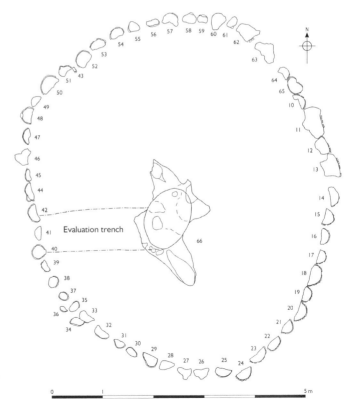

(Above) The evaluation trench, running from the central tree to Timber 41, revealed a great deal about the construction of the monument and provided valuable clues about its age.

(Right) Detailed plan of the timber circle, including the numbers given to the individual timbers.

N

Evaluation trench

66

0   1   5 m

A laser-scan of one of the timbers from the Holme circle, showing the evidence that enabled the archaeologists to make a detailed analysis of the axe-marks on the timbers.

ring of posts to the central tree, and one outside the ring to search for traces of an external ring-ditch. Such ring-ditches often surround Bronze Age 'barrows' or funerary mounds. The trench inside the ring of timbers was about one metre deep and slightly more than shoulder-width across. At its outer end, on the western side of the circle, the trench exposed the inner face of Timber 41, chosen because it seemed reasonably typical of all the posts, plus a couple of inches of the posts on either side.

One of the first things the trial excavation revealed, however, was that the term 'post' was a misleading one. On the surface, the circle looked like a ring of free-standing posts, but it soon became clear that the timbers had been skilfully split and positioned to butt up tightly against one another, giving the structure much greater strength and a distinctive, 'wall of wood' appearance. The reason the timbers looked like posts above the surface was simply that the waves and sand had stripped away the bark and soft, outer wood, leaving only the harder wood at the heart of the timbers. Even this 'heartwood' was peppered with tiny holes originally made by piddocks (a type of burrowing mollusc), then populated by worms and other marine life.

Timber 41 and the exposed side of the central tree, however, yielded much more than a collection of fascinating sea creatures. Below ground the wood

had suffered no erosion and the trench revealed that Timber 41 was half – vertically split – of the trunk of a young oak tree, with its bark on the outside of the circle. (Fingertip inspection of the other timbers, going only a few inches deep, showed that 54 of the 55 peripheral timbers had also been positioned to show bark on the outside of the circle.) Although Timber 41 was left in position during the trial excavation, so only its inward-facing side could be closely examined, it seemed to have been about 50 years old when the tree was felled and its straightness hinted that it might have come from a fast-growing tree in an area where the taller, older trees had been cleared. The bottom of the timber, meanwhile, had an off-centre V-shaped tip, suggesting that the tree had been carefully felled. (It was clear to Maisie Taylor, the team's expert on prehistoric wood, that the V-shape was not the result of sharpening the timber to drive it into the ground, but was the 'felling step' inadvertently created when the tree was cut down. By cutting a tree on opposite sides, it is possible to control where it will fall – the V-shape of Timber 41 would have resulted from the tree's subsequently being split in half at right-angles to the thin 'hinge' of wood between the two cuts.)

At the other end of the trial trench was more evidence of the workmanship of the builders of the timber circle. To everyone's surprise, the bark had been removed from the central tree and, more exciting still, axe-marks were clearly visible on the trunk. To Maisie Taylor these marks were strong evidence that the bark had been stripped off during the Bronze Age. Further, the curvature and width of the axe blades hinted at a Bronze Age date.

The evidence was tantalising. The neat splitting and the tell-tale V-shaped tip of Timber 41, the de-barking of the central tree trunk and the axe-marks preserved on its surface all promised to reveal a great deal about Bronze Age tree-felling and woodworking techniques. But what did these things *mean*? Why were the split timbers in the ring all – except one – arranged with their bark facing outwards? Why was the central tree planted upside-down? Why did the builders of the circle strip the bark from the tree's trunk?

Perhaps de-barking it was a practical woodworking matter, and a de-barked tree stump was easier to shape and manoeuvre than one with its bark intact. Or perhaps there was a deeper significance, and the removal of the bark was a symbol of purification. A full excavation of the Holme timber circle might provide answers to these and other questions, and shine new light on Bronze Age culture and beliefs.

For now, however, there was a trial excavation to complete. Only once the investigation was over and the reports were written could English Heritage assess the site and decide what to do next.

The second trench, outside the circle, had revealed disturbed ground to the north of the circle, but no clear evidence of a ring-ditch, so there was little more to be done. In any case, as winter approached, the tides and the onshore winds were changing, leaving shorter and shorter windows of opportunity between tides for the team to prolong

the trial excavation. There was just one job left: taking samples from the central tree and four of the surrounding posts for dendrochronological dating (that is, dating by scientific analysis of the timbers' growth rings). At that point, a full excavation was not being considered, so the

Three's a crowd: Maisie Taylor, the expert on prehistoric wood and co-founder of the Flag Fen Bronze Age centre, joins two members of the Norfolk Archaeological Unit in the evaluation trench.

samples were taken with a chainsaw – this was the quickest, most efficient way to obtain samples large enough for the dendrologists to work on. No one thought twice about it. The damage done to the timbers, however – especially to the central tree, which suffered a deep gash – was later spotted by protesters and by the media, and the chainsaw 'incident' became one of the most controversial episodes in the Seahenge story.

That was in the future, however. Once the samples had been taken, the team cleared the site, packed up their equipment, and left. The trial excavation was finished.

THE BRONZE AGE

In recent years our view of the Bronze Age has changed enormously. In the 'Three Age System' introduced in the 19th century the Bronze Age in Britain was an arbitrary period spanning the 2,000 years, approximately, between 2500 BC and 500 BC. Its beginning was marked by the arrival of metal – specifically copper and bronze – and its end by the transition from bronze to iron.

New discoveries and new perspectives, however, show that the reality was far more complex. As archaeologist Martyn Barber says in his book *Bronze and the Bronze Age*, 'There

was no clear break in cultural or economic life, no mass incursion of pots and their makers. Indeed, there is nothing in the archaeological record – no change in artefact styles, in monument types, in modes of subsistence or settlement, in burial rites – that can clearly be attributed to the arrival and establishment in the British Isles of metalworking. That change occurred is undeniable, but the processes that brought it about appear far more elusive and complex than, say, invasion, and were of the long-term rather than overnight variety.'

So what was this phase in Britain's history really like?

Population estimates vary, but a 'rough and ready guess' by archaeologist Francis Pryor puts the figures at 250,000 in about 2000 BC, growing to 500,000 by 1000 BC. These people were shorter than modern Britons, largely due to poorer nutrition, but in other ways were quite similar to us. They may have been tattooed, for example, and were concerned about their clothes and personal appearance. They made buttons from plain and semiprecious stones, and jewellery from bronze and gold; they pinned fabric in place with straight pins fashioned from bone or metal; men often shaved their faces, while many women wore skilfully knotted hairnets; and, towards the end of the period at least, Bronze Age Britons were spinning thread to produce woven and patterned fabrics.

They also built substantial 'roundhouses', typically from 5m to 10m (c 16ft to 33ft) in diameter. (Evidence of settlements in Norfolk is rare, however, partly because timber and daub houses leave very little trace for archaeologists, but also because stock keeping and sheep-herding entailed a mobile lifestyle.) The wheel made its first appearance in Britain during the Bronze Age.

Agriculture became firmly established, with land clearance increasing and accelerating and people

The Egtved girl: the well-preserved clothes (including a top, a belt and a knotted-string skirt) of a Bronze Age girl buried in an oak-trunk coffin in Egtved, Denmark.

accumulating wealth through animals. At the same time, social and religious changes were taking place. There were more individual, high-status burials, suggesting the existence of a rich and powerful elite, and the burials were mainly of men, which suggests a patriarchal society. Excavated burial mounds have also produced evidence that some people met violent deaths.

As well as wealth, status and violence, however, culture was an important element of Bronze Age life. Metalworking and other decorative styles show that there was regular contact with the continent, and the characteristic 'Beaker' style of pottery, strongly associated with the Low Countries, was widespread in Britain during the Early Bronze Age.

(Below) Reconstruction of a Bronze Age roundhouse at Flag Fen in Cambridgeshire

(Above) The oldest wheel in Britain, excavated at Flag Fen and dating to the Bronze Age.

The prehistoric environment at Holme

In January 1999 the preliminary dendrochronology dates were in. The analysis had been carried out at Sheffield University, where the team determined that the central oak tree and the four timbers had almost certainly been felled at approximately the same time. The central tree was 167 years old at that time, and the four posts somewhat younger, their ages ranging from 89 to 128 years. The dendrochronologists were not yet able to say approximately in which year the trees had been felled, however – that information would be teased out of the ancient timbers some time later, with a degree of precision that caught almost everyone by surprise.

Already there were reasonably strong indications that the timber circle dated back to the Bronze Age, so the archaeologists at Norfolk Archaeological Unit and English Heritage waited patiently for a firm date from the dendrochronologists in Sheffield. In the mean time, they had begun to focus on another question: if the circle was really so old, how had it survived for several thousand years?

The answer, although only a tentative one at this stage, lay in a brief report prepared by Peter Murphy, the English Heritage adviser for archaeological science for eastern England.

As part of the evaluation, he examined the prehistoric environment of the Holme beach site.

As sea levels rose, the tides stripped away layers of sand and peat, finally exposing the timber circle to the elements again in 1998.

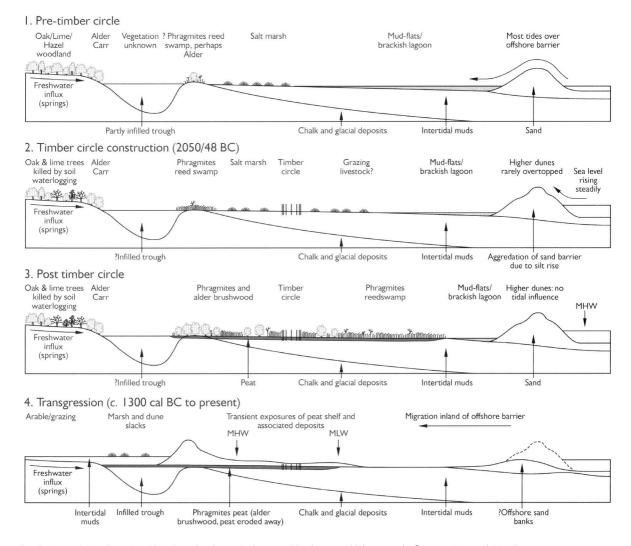

1. Pre-timber circle

Oak/Lime/Hazel woodland | Alder Carr | Vegetation unknown | ? Phragmites reed swamp, perhaps Alder | Salt marsh | Mud-flats/brackish lagoon | Most tides over offshore barrier

Freshwater influx (springs)

Partly infilled trough   Chalk and glacial deposits   Intertidal muds   Sand

2. Timber circle construction (2050/48 BC)

Oak & lime trees killed by soil waterlogging | Alder Carr | Phragmites reed swamp | Salt marsh | Timber circle | Grazing livestock? | Mud-flats/brackish lagoon | Higher dunes rarely overtopped | Sea level rising steadily

Freshwater influx (springs)

?Infilled trough   Chalk and glacial deposits   Intertidal muds   Aggregation of sand barrier due to silt rise

3. Post timber circle

Oak & lime trees killed by soil waterlogging | Alder Carr | Phragmites and alder brushwood | Timber circle | Phragmites reedswamp | Mud-flats/brackish lagoon | Higher dunes: no tidal influence

MHW

Freshwater influx (springs)

?Infilled trough   Peat   Chalk and glacial deposits   Intertidal muds   Sand

4. Transgression (c. 1300 cal BC to present)

Arable/grazing | Marsh and dune slacks | Transient exposures of peat shelf and associated deposits | Migration inland of offshore barrier

MHW   MLW

Freshwater influx (springs)

Intertidal muds | Infilled trough | Phragmites peat (alder brushwood, peat eroded away) | Chalk and glacial deposits | Intertidal muds | ?Offshore sand banks

Landscape evolution: illustrations that show the change in the coastal landscape at Holme-next-the-Sea over time, explaining how the timber circle was preserved for so long and why it finally reappeared in 1998.

The fragmentary peat beds visible on the beach suggested that at one time the area had been an inland marsh, criss-crossed by streams and populated with rushes, lime and alder trees. Further, the freshwater flora and fauna in the peat and in the sediment below hinted that the marsh was protected from the open sea by a barrier of sand and gravel, perhaps not unlike today's sand dunes. Also, analysis carried out elsewhere on the north Norfolk coast showed that the peat had been formed during the Bronze Age. However, when exactly had the circle been built? If the environment had been a swampy one (with a high groundwater table) when the builders were erecting the circle, then the posts would almost certainly have been dropped into a water-filled construction trench, which would explain their remarkable state of preservation. The crucial question – which Peter Murphy would later be able to answer – was whether the circle was built before, during or after the time that the inland marsh environment existed.

Media frenzy: the press scents a big story

The issue facing English Heritage, which had funded the evaluation of the Holme timber circle, was whether to go ahead with a full excavation. There was no question that the monument was at risk. Without the protective peat layer, the oxygen-free conditions that had preserved the circle for so long had been breached. The beach was becoming steeper and the wave action more powerful; salts in the brine were attacking the wood, and there was a further risk from wood-boring molluscs and marine microbes.

Paradoxically, there was also a danger from dehydration as the timbers were exposed to the air

Scant defence: a sign reminds visitors that their very presence is a threat to a sensitive ecosystem.

between tides. As most of the cellulose – which gives wood its strength – had been lost over the millennia, the timbers would simply have disintegrated if they had been allowed to dry out without proper treatment. Without a full excavation, one of Britain's most exciting archaeological finds of the late 20th century would soon be lost.

It was clear, however, that not only would a full-scale excavation in an intertidal zone be very expensive, but it would also be enormously difficult, as the work would at the mercy of the tides. An excavation would also pose a significant threat to the fragile ecosystem of the Holme Dunes reserve. So English Heritage had three options: they could somehow preserve the circle where it stood, they could excavate the timbers and preserve them elsewhere, or they could make a full record of the site and abandon the monument to the waves. It was an unenviable choice.

So far, the debate had been conducted exclusively among the archaeological community. In December 1998 the site was featured in *British Archaeology*, the magazine of the Council for British Archaeology. A local news agency then picked up on the discovery and tried to distribute the story, but with little success – BBC Radio Norfolk ran a brief news item, but almost immediately lost interest. Apart from these two brief reports, the Holme timber circle had received very little public attention.

On Saturday 9 January the peace was shattered. 'Shifting sands yield "Stonehenge of the sea"' ran the headline on a front-page article in *The Independent*. The paper's environment correspondent, Michael McCarthy, had seen the feature in *British Archaeology* and knew a good story when he saw one. His report quoted Mark Brennand: 'I really do find it eerie and profoundly moving. All the hard-bitten archaeologists who saw it out there felt the same'; and Dr Francis Pryor, President of the Council for British Archaeology, who said, 'I was staggered when I first saw it. I had goose pimples. It really was like stepping back 4,000 years. It's unique. It is of enormous international importance.' McCarthy also reported that, for Dr Pryor, the timber circle was the most extraordinary archaeological discovery and it had to be preserved.

Shifting sands yield 'Stonehenge of the sea'

The mysterious 'tree temple' on the north Norfolk coast. Unless action is taken the 4,000-year-old circle may disappear for ever   *Mark Brennand/Norfolk Archaeology Unit*

BY MICHAEL McCARTHY,
Environment Correspondent

It is one of the eeriest and most mysterious ancient monuments discovered in Britain.

A massive oak tree, stuck into the ground upside down with its great spread of roots pointing skywards, stands surrounded by a palisade-like circle of oak trunks. And it has just emerged from the sea.

A wooden relative of Stonehenge, thought to be some sort of altar, it has just been revealed by the shifting sands of Norfolk, where it had lain buried and preserved for thousands of years. A beachcomber alerted archaeologists, who started excavating in October.

The site, on the lonely coast at Holme-next-the-Sea near Hunstanton, is almost certainly ritual and probably to do with death. Within its oval ring of 54 posts is the inverted oak tree with its roots, "like a table with fingers," says Dr Francis Pryor, President of the Council for British Archaeology. He believes it is very likely to have been some form of altar.

The tree-temple – if that is what it is – has been uncovered by tidal erosion. It is thought to have been constructed in the early Bronze Age, between 2000 and 1200 BC, which would make it almost a contemporary of Stonehenge.

The site, says Dr Pryor, is the most extraordinary archaeological discovery he has ever seen and it must be preserved. "I was staggered when I first saw it," he said. "I had goose pimples. It really was like stepping back 4,000 years. It's unique. It is of enormous international importance."

But unless difficult decisions are taken soon about preserving it, it is likely to be destroyed by the action of the tides within two years. No decision can be made until the site is precisely dated. Carbon dating of the wood is being carried out.

An excavation led by Mark Brennand of Norfolk County Council's Archaeological Unit suggests that the tree-temple was constructed on swampy ground some way inland, which the sea covered at a later date.

Mr Brennand believes the purpose of the site was probably excarnation – the practice of exposing bodies of the dead so that the flesh rotted more quickly, thus, it was thought, speeding the spirit on its way to the afterlife. "I really do find it eerie, and profoundly moving," he said. "All the hard-bitten archaeologists who saw it out there felt the same. You're directly in the presence of the past at a very personal level."

Dr Pryor added that for our ancestors, oak was a special wood: "The inverted oak is not just utilitarian, a simple way of making an altar. It is a very complex symbolic statement. Perhaps a little sinister. It is the world turned upside down."

Suddenly, the debate was in the public domain. *The Independent*'s use of the word 'Stonehenge' in its headline had suggested that the Holme circle might be a comparable national treasure, even through it was in fact far smaller. (Michael McCarthy's report made no mention of the circle's dimensions, and the photograph gave no clue to its scale.) Nor was it a true henge – although the word derives from the 'hanging' stones at Stonehenge, the term is now used by archaeologists to describe a circular earthwork of a bank and ditch. The trial excavation produced no evidence for either type of structure; and while henge

The Independent's front-page story on Saturday, 9 January 1999: suddenly the debate over excavation was in the public arena.

(Overleaf) The north Norfolk coast, looking eastward, from the air; the timber circle and two archaeologists' vehicles are visible near the bottom of the photograph.

earthworks have sometimes been found to contain circles of free-standing posts, the timbers of the Holme circle formed a solid wall.

No matter. The next to enter the discussion was the regional daily newspaper, the *Eastern Daily Press*. On Monday 11 January it ran a two-page feature under the banner headline 'Our Stonehenge beneath the sea', the next day it fanned the flames with a piece headlined 'Preservation of circle "is not possible"', and on Thursday 14 January it produced a 'Norfolk's Seahenge' souvenir pullout in which one headline asked 'The big question is: should it be saved?'

Now the monument had a catchy, if inappropriate, new name and, as Francis Pryor wrote later in his book *Seahenge: A Quest for Life and Death in Bronze Age Britain*, 'All hell broke loose. To say that the media picked up the story would be a gross understatement. They picked it up, ran with it, tossed it around in the air, and devoured it. Archaeological web sites were jammed with people demanding that something be done to save the timbers from the sea.'

The archaeologists, however, no longer had the field to themselves. Many local people felt that *they* were the natural custodians of the circle and that it should be left in peace. New Agers and druids claimed a kind of spiritual ownership of the circle, and they wanted to save it from what they saw as a violation. 'Let's put a dome over it with a tunnel under the beach,' said New Age protester Buster Nolan with more than a hint of sarcasm. 'Whatever it costs, it will be worth the money. People will come from all over the world to see that.'

On the other side of the fence were the regional tourism organisations, who saw the timber circle as an opportunity. 'A structure of this importance cannot be allowed to disappear,' argued Geoff Skipper, Tourism Development Officer for Norwich, 'because it would be a major draw for people from all over the country.'

Then there were the regular users of Holme beach. Some wanted the timber circle excavated and preserved, while others were happy for it to be left to its 'natural' fate. They were all taken aback by the furore. 'I've never seen so many people here before,' said regular dog-walker Katherine Ramsay. 'Normally it's a wonderfully empty, windswept beach.' It was this dramatic increase in visitor numbers that concerned the Norfolk Wildlife Trust, whose Holme Dunes National Nature Reserve included the beach down to the low-water line. In the first three months of 1999, more than 5,000 people had visited the beach to see the now-famous 'Seahenge' timber circle.

'People coming to see the monument will soon destroy it,' said Gary Hibberd, Warden of the Holme Dunes reserve, to an interviewer. 'As we are walking now, we are disturbing feeding waders, and that will be constant if visitors come here in any numbers. I hope they are going to preserve the environment. I hope they are going to take Seahenge away.'

The decision makers at English Heritage faced a very difficult choice indeed.

Oystercatchers nesting in the sand dunes at Holme Dunes reserve.

Should the circle be excavated?

In its feature headlined 'Preservation of circle "is not possible"' on Tuesday 12 January, the *Eastern Daily Press* had quoted Geoffrey Wainwright, Chief Archaeologist for English Heritage, as saying, 'At the moment the archaeological work is a recording exercise. What is not possible is preserving it in its present position.' He did not go as far as saying that the timber circle could not be removed from the beach at Holme and preserved somewhere else, but that seemed to be the message to anyone reading between the lines.

One reason for English Heritage's apparent reluctance to excavate was cost. Norfolk County Council had shown no enthusiasm to fund even the trial excavation, and the Norfolk Museum Service, which itself was funded by the county council, was also unable to help. If there was to be a full excavation, English Heritage would have to foot the bill.

How much was it likely to cost? The answer was revealed in a letter from Sir Jocelyn Stevens, then Chairman of English Heritage, to Philip Carr-Gomm, an otherwise uninvolved private individual who had e-mailed Sir Jocelyn on the future of the Holme circle. 'We are considering the possibility of preserving the circle,' wrote the Chairman, 'but that option presents a number of difficulties, not least because the timbers are submerged by the sea for up to 23 hours each day. The likelihood of being able to preserve the circle where it stands is remote and we can see little point in doing so. The second option is to lift the timbers, conserve them and re-erect the monument on terra firma at a suitable location. This would be a major operation which preliminary estimates of cost put at 500K.'

The Chairman went on to say that his organisation was 'exploring the preservation options whilst we await the dating of the timbers', but his main point was already clear: £500,000 was a lot of money to find, especially at such short notice.

The pressure continued to mount, however. Many members of the public and opinion-formers in the media were horrified that such a significant find might be left to erode away, and they were backed to the hilt by a strong majority of the archaeological community and by English Nature and the Norfolk Wildlife Trust, both of which were anxious to minimise damage and disruption at the Holme Dunes reserve. If English Heritage chose to leave the Holme circle to the elements, there would be uproar.

Opinions were changing behind the scenes, however, and, on 16 March 1999, Dr Francis Pryor, President of the Council for British Archaeology and an expert on the Bronze Age, received a phone call from Geoffrey Wainwright at English Heritage. The decision to excavate and remove the timbers had been made, he said, and if the Fenland Archaeological Trust (co-founded by Dr Pryor in 1987) was willing, they would initially be held and treated at the Trust's field centre at Flag Fen in Cambridgeshire.

Was the Fenland Archaeological Trust willing? It was, with no hesitation whatsoever – and the stage was set for a dramatic and exciting summer.

3 Excavation

At work on the beach: tides, crabs and mud

The team from the Norfolk Archaeological Unit arrived at Holme beach on Wednesday 26 May 1999. Mark Brennand was again site director and Maisie Taylor the expert on prehistoric waterlogged wood, but this time the team included seven more full-time archaeologists. Bronze Age specialist Francis Pryor was frequently on site, too, while back in Norwich Bill Boismier took on the role of project manager. Despite the fuss in the media and the daunting challenge of excavating a timber circle between tides that would submerge the monument beneath the North Sea twice a day, the mood was one of excitement. For Mark, Maisie and the other team members – David Adams, Fran Green, Steve Hickling, Barry Martin, Neil Moss, Simon Underdown and Pete Warsop of NAU, plus occasional volunteers John Ames, Helen Evans and Duncan Stirk – this would be the project of a lifetime.

What added to the sense of excitement was the certainty that the timber circle dated back to the Bronze Age. Although the dendrochronologists were still at work and had yet to deliver precise details, they had confirmed that the wood was more than 4,000 years old.

The first task was to remove the sand and silt that had been deposited within the circle by the sluggish summer tides. As the team got to work, it slowly became clear exactly how big a job they had taken on. Not only did the tide tables and onshore breezes restrict them to periods of between two and four hours per day – and no hours per day on quite a few occasions – but also the first hour or two every day was spent digging, baling and pumping out the water and silt washed in by the previous tide.

(Above) Baling out: the first job each day was to bale and pump water out of the circle, so digging could begin.

(Right) One of the many crabs resident in the peat on Holme beach in 1999.

Water and silt were not the only things the team found on site when they arrived each day. The part-excavated circle acted as an unintended fish trap as the tide receded, and there would often be eels, flatfish and pipefish in the trench dug the day before, not to mention the ever-present crabs, which rewarded the archaeologists with many a painful nip. On one occasion, the circle was even filled with baby lobsters; but there were always crabs. Over time it became a daily ritual to gather the crabs in a bucket at the start of each day's work and release them farther down the beach.

Because the excavation was unlike anything the team had done before, there were some important decisions to be taken about how work would proceed and how the fragile, 4,000-year-old timbers would be handled. First, the archaeologists placed a ring of sandbags around the circle, to minimise the amount of sand and silt washed back in by the tides, and to enable the pumping-out to begin as soon as the tide had retreated – but how to lift the timbers? Each one was not only extremely delicate, but also completely waterlogged and very heavy. The priority was the condition of the timbers, so Mark Brennand decided that he and his team would excavate and

No time to waste: to achieve as much as possible in the short time available between tides, the team would begin work each day before the sea had retreated beyond the timber circle.

Recording the facts on the ground: at every stage of the excavation, careful drawings were made of the exact positions of the timbers.

raise the timbers in the circle by hand. Only the central oak tree – which later proved to weigh almost two tons – would be lifted by crane.

The team knew that normal archaeological techniques were not going to be easy to follow, as the changes in soil colour normally used as a guide by archaeologists were not visible on the surface of the mud inside the circle. However, they also knew that the posts (which had not been sharpened) had not been driven into the ground – the builders must have excavated a trench, placed the posts in it and then back-filled around them. This back-filled material had been exposed at the time of construction, and could have contained all sorts of information about the circle and about the Bronze Age environment. So it was extremely important to identify and sample it.

For the digging itself the team worked to a series of cross-sections visible in the sides of trenches dug between the ring of timbers and a notional 'island' of silt surrounding the central tree. Two trenches were opened on opposing sides of the circle. At the

Each timber, apart from the central oak stump, was carefully removed by hand and carried from the site on a canvas stretcher.

circumference of the circle, each successive trench exposed two timbers; while the timbers were still in place, the archaeologists made an accurate drawing of the long, clean-cut side of the trench, and took soil samples. Then the timbers themselves were eased away from the silt outside the circle – no easy task, as the vacuum-like seal had to be broken – and manoeuvred onto a canvas stretcher. Finally, the two timbers from each 'radial' trench were loaded on to a trailer and driven to the Bronze Age centre at Flag Fen for cleaning and conservation. Once a trench had been documented and the timbers removed, it was extended to take in the next timbers.

(Overleaf) In the public eye: the media attention ensured that the archaeologists almost always had an audience.

Deciding to excavate the timber circle by hand was a courageous decision – although it meant harder, more painstaking work for the archaeologists, it also guaranteed that the timbers and the information they contained would be preserved in the best possible condition.

The first timber to be lifted gave the team a good idea of what lay ahead. On Friday 28 May, having been repulsed by the tide and a strong onshore breeze the day before, they had finished sampling and recording the trench, and were ready to lift the 250lb (113.4kg) timber, when it slipped and trapped Mark Brennand's foot. 'I knew it was heavy,' he told the *Eastern Daily Press* later, 'but not that heavy. It pinned me down for a while, but there was no harm done.'

At this point in the excavation, the focus was on documenting the site, raising the timbers safely and taking samples. The detailed analysis would come later. None the less, the team was intrigued by the things they were finding. For example, many of the timbers contained clear axe-marks, and buried around some of the timbers were piles of woodworking debris.

Geoff Needham (left), Chairman of Holme-next-the-Sea Parish Council, and David Miles, Chief Archaeologist, English Heritage.

Also, among the timbers used for the circle were 'roundwood' (that is, complete, unsplit trunks), half-split timbers and other, less-neatly-split wood; but all the timbers except one were placed with their bark facing outwards. Did this mean something? If so, what? And why was the central tree in the ground upside down? Was something – or someone – buried underneath it?

The fascinating questions were piling up.

Leave it alone! The protesters speak up

Prior to the excavation, the controversy about the site had been gathering new force, too. At the beginning of May, English Heritage had announced its decision to go ahead with a full-scale excavation, and suddenly the dynamics of the situation changed. While the media had earlier reported on the battle to get English Heritage to fund the excavation and preservation of the Holme timber circle, now the focus was on the protesters' attempts to shut the project down. The colour and range of the objections – from villagers and spiritualists to druids and environmentalists – made it easy to keep the story running, and high-profile press coverage, plus phone-ins and opinion polls on radio and television, inflamed passions further.

In the village of Holme-next-the Sea itself opinions were divided, but the anti-excavation group had a formidable leader in Geoff Needham, a former fisherman and now Chairman of the Parish Council. He and many others in the village wanted to preserve their local heritage and felt ignored by English Heritage. They were not alone. The more publicity the story received, the more people spoke up, in Norfolk and elsewhere.

Days before the excavation was due to start, the archaeologists arranged a public meeting for Tuesday 25 May, which English Heritage agreed to attend. Well aware of the raging debate in the media – indeed, it was impossible not to be aware of it – English Heritage also tried to calm things down by issuing a statement confirming that once the timber circle had been cleaned and conserved, it would be displayed somewhere in west Norfolk. But the statement did not have the desired effect on the villagers of Holme. 'We thought they'd called the meeting finally to listen to what we've got to say,' said Geoff Needham at the time. 'Now it turns out that they've already made up their minds.'

The meeting at Holme village hall was tense and sometimes angry. English Heritage and the Norfolk archaeologists explained their view that the excavation was an unprecedented chance to learn more about the Early Bronze Age in Britain. Moreover, if the timbers were not lifted and preserved now, they would be lost forever to the sea as the beach at Holme continued to steepen. Some local people, though, felt that they knew the beach better than anyone, while others thought the structure could and should be preserved *in situ*, or be allowed to decay *in situ*. Nearly all were contemptuous of the use of a chainsaw (the words 'vandalism' and 'desecration' were frequently used) during the autumn evaluation to take a sample of the central tree for dating purposes.

Everyone felt poorly treated by officialdom.

Although there was a frank exchange of views and everyone had their say, the meeting ended with no resolution to any of the big issues. The excavation was still scheduled to begin the next day.

The archaeologists arrived as planned, and soon had their first taste of what was to come. From the outset, Geoff Needham was present with his video camera, determined to record events at the site. On Thursday 27 May he was joined by conservationist Buster Nolan, who read poetry and blasted the team with his didgeridoo. 'Seahenge has more meaning and power on the beach here at Holme than it does anywhere else,' he told the eager reporter from the *Eastern Daily Press*, who probably could not believe his luck. 'This is 60 grand being spent by archaeologists who are patting each other on the back, telling each other they're doing the right thing. It's a farce.'

Protester Buster Nolan shares his views with a member of the Norfolk Archaeological Unit.

In one sense he was right: events on the beach did, at times, resemble a farce. Other protesters joined the regulars, some for a single day, others for as many days as they could manage. While some remonstrated with the archaeologists, others stayed silent. One protester, Des Crow, began dismantling the wall of sandbags one day, and switched off the pump that kept the circle free of water. Often a couple of police officers were present, although theirs was mainly a watching brief, to ensure things did not turn nasty.

The media, of course, were always on hand to record every word.

Brian Ayers, County Archaeologist for Norfolk, gives the archaeologists' point of view in a television interview.

After more than a week of this, Buster Nolan went to a local firm of solicitors to try to get the courts to put a stop to the excavation. Although the various protests had slowed things down, it was clear that time was on the archaeologists' side, so a legal solution seemed the protesters' best hope of success. Behind him, Nolan had the promise of financial support from the Council of British Druid Orders and, more meaningfully, £2,000 from Mervyn Lambert, a south Norfolk businessman who had followed the saga of the timber circle in the press. 'The people of Norfolk should have more balls,' Lambert told the *Eastern Daily Press*. 'I'm amazed they're allowing it to happen. I'm not mega-rich, but I feel that if money can be used to protect Norfolk's heritage, then I will have done my bit for future generations. I'm not usually in much sympathy with druids and hippies, but I believe they are more in touch with nature than the rest of us. I'd go up there to Holme with the hippies and blow a didgeridoo with them, if I didn't have this plant-hire business to run.'

Throughout the on-site shenanigans the archaeologists' approach was to remain calm and courteous, to continue the excavation and to explain their work to interested observers. One member of the team was always available to discuss the project with the public and the media.

Graham Johnston, cameraman for Channel 4's Time Team, *had full, fly-on-the-wall access to the excavation.*

No matter what the weather was like during the excavation, the archaeologists got on with the job, and a steady flow of onlookers stopped by to look.

Archaeologists discuss on-site security with a local policeman.

Meanwhile, Buster Nolan's attempt to halt the excavation by legal means ground swiftly to a halt, as the solicitors were not prepared to take the case on. Not only did English Heritage have the resources to fight the case effectively, they thought, but it was an arm of government and would have much greater credibility in court than the druids. Further, the circle had no legal protection, and the excavation was being undertaken with the landowner's permission. The protesters' case seemed to be a lost cause. So the heckling protests continued and, during the second week of June, Mark Brennand and his team began making plans to lift the central tree. Fourteen timbers from the circle had been removed by now, and there was room for a small crane to get close enough to raise the tree safely.

The date was set: Tuesday 15 June.

On the day, the full Seahenge circus was in attendance. The archaeologists had been joined by officials from English Heritage and the local council; the police and the media were watching carefully; birdwatchers and strollers were drawn to the unusual group of people and vehicles on the beach; the diggers whose hydraulic arms would lift the tree were ready and waiting; and the circle itself was full of protesters. There was even a brightly-painted World War II landing craft on the scene. No one knew what would happen, and the mood was tense – but in the end, there were no fireworks. Despite repeated appeals from the police and from David Miles, Chief Archaeologist at English Heritage, the protesters simply refused to move. It was stalemate. The lifting was off and the diggers retreated along the beach.

'Showdown at Seahenge', read the headline on page three of the Eastern Daily Press the next day. Although the national media were not reporting the excavation and protests daily, the regional newspapers, television and radio were; and the plucky-locals-take-on-government-agency tone of some of the coverage encouraged more people to voice their opposition to the removal of the timber circle.

To counter this turn of events, English Heritage suspended the excavation and proposed a meeting of all interested parties. The suspension happened at an awkward time for the archaeologists, however, as one post had been left exposed at the end of an open trench and could have been damaged, or even washed away, by the swirling tide. The solution was to mount a dawn raid, arriving silently at Holme beach in the early hours of Friday 18 June to lift the exposed post. But while the post was saved, the protesters were enraged when they discovered that the suspension had been breached. Immediately before a meeting intended to bring the two sides closer together, the little goodwill that remained was disappearing fast.

Rollo Maughfling, Archdruid of Stonehenge and Glastonbury, on top of the central tree stump.

The meeting took place on Tuesday 22 June, exactly a week after the aborted lifting of the central tree, at the Le Strange Arms Hotel in nearby Hunstanton. Present were representatives of English Heritage, Norfolk Archaeological Unit, Norfolk Wildlife Trust, the villagers of Holme-next-the-Sea and the protesters, and the meeting was chaired by spiritualist Clare Prout. During the five-hour meeting, a 'talking stick' was passed from speaker to speaker, with no one permitted to interrupt the holder.

Talking stick or no talking stick, little was achieved at the Hunstanton meeting. The attendees did agree on general points such as their concern for the wildlife, the vulnerability of the beach, and the sacredness of the site both to those who built it and to a number of people today. Some protesters, however, Des Crow among them, later took issue with the minutes of the meeting, which implied agreement from all parties that the excavation should continue from 28 June. After Hunstanton, the two sides were as far apart as ever.

At the end of June, the excavation began again, and although the police had expected the number of protesters to grow, in fact the numbers declined. Buster Nolan and Des Crow were regularly on the beach, but few others were present and the archaeologists were able to make progress. But the spectacle was not over yet. Buster Nolan had contacted Rollo Maughfling, the Archdruid of Stonehenge and Glastonbury, who duly arrived at Holme-next-the-Sea on the morning of Thursday 1 July. Asserting his 'common law rights of religious assembly granted by King Richard in 1189', the Archdruid waded across the circle to the inverted roots of the central oak tree, clambered up, and delivered an eight-point proclamation.

Although this was the most confrontational day since the attempted lifting of the central tree more than two weeks earlier, Mark Brennand's team kept their heads down and got on with the job. Around them the protesters objected loudly, photographers' cameras flashed, journalists took notes and spoke jauntily into microphones, dog-walkers stopped by for a look, and the police stood ready to intervene. For all concerned, it was business as usual.

The next day, however, events took a new turn. To try to put an end to the protests, which had caused the excavation to fall way behind schedule, English Heritage had obtained an interim injunction against Des Crow, Rollo Maughfling, Geoff Needham, Buster Nolan and 'John Doe', which banned them from the site. Under the terms of the injunction, if they interfered with the excavation, they could be arrested and charged with a criminal offence. Further, 'John Doe' was a legal construct that applied to any other person who attempted to obstruct the excavation. If the injunction was upheld, the protests were over.

The protesters had not been expecting a legal measure like this from English Heritage, but they responded fast. Once again, businessman Mervyn Lambert stepped in to offer financial support, and the four named individuals went to the county court to defend themselves. The judge agreed that there was a case to be heard, and the hearing was set for the following Tuesday, 6 July, at the Royal Courts of Justice in London.

Unearthing the Bronze Age

When the lifted timbers arrived at the Flag Fen field centre in Cambridgeshire, usually two at a time, Maisie Taylor and her team first cleaned the mud off them, slowly and with great care, and then were able to examine them for the first time in greater detail. Mark Brennand and his fellow archaeologists from the Norfolk Archaeological Unit would join the analytical and interpretive work once the excavation was finished at Holme, but for now Maisie and her colleagues had the timbers to themselves.

From their examination of the site, the lifted timbers and the many soil and other samples, Mark, Maisie and the team hoped to discover who had built the structure, how they had built it, what it might have looked like originally, why it had been built in this particular location and whether there was any special significance in the arrangement of the posts. They also wanted to learn exactly why the timber circle was so well preserved, to help understand how best to preserve it for the

(Top) Two timbers in situ, exposed and ready for removal later the same day.

(Above) Individual timbers from Holme-next-the-Sea in holding tanks at Flag Fen.

future. At last, they could begin teasing some answers out of the ancient, waterlogged wood.

The central tree and the 55 timbers surrounding it were all oak. But not the sort of oak the autumn evaluation of the site had led Maisie to expect. At the outer end of the trial trench, the one exposed timber – Timber 41 – had been good, straight wood that appeared to have come from a fast-growing tree. Everyone expected that it would be typical of the group of timbers as a whole. It was not. Instead, the other timbers that came into Flag Fen were mostly knotted, gnarly wood that must have been tough for the Bronze Age builders to work. Why had they used such poor-quality timber? Most likely because it was the best they could find near by. After all, the circle had been constructed in a low-lying marshland, the sort of environment that produces oak trees that grow slowly, with only short distances along their trunks between branches. It was probably easier to work with low-grade oak such as this than to haul better specimens to the site from farther afield.

It was also possible to imagine more clearly the timber circle above ground. On the beach, the timbers had all been about 1m (c 3ft 3in) deep in the grey mud, and it is very unlikely that the ground level 4,000 years earlier was any lower. This depth suggests that up to 3–4m (c 10–13ft) of the posts could have protruded and remained stable above ground. The nature of the gnarly wood makes 3m (c 10ft) lengths more likely.

So the structure could easily have stood taller than the people who built it and, given the lack of a sufficiently tall central support, it was unlikely to have had a roof.

Contrary to initial impressions, however, it did appear to have an entrance. Two of the timbers, numbers 35 and 37, turned out to be forked branches of the same trunk or branch – the forked gap, although only eight inches or so wide, was the only access or view into the finished circle. Strangely,

A reconstruction painting, by artist Judith Dobie, of how the finished timber circle might have looked.

45

though, the entrance was blocked on the outside by a post, Timber 36, that had been driven about 0.5 m (c 1 ft 7 in) into the ground immediately in front of the gap. Further, the 'blocking post' came from the same tree as some of the timbers in the circle, so it was likely to have been inserted at the same time.

Had this post been driven into the ground after someone had entered or left the circle, or was it purley symbolic? The gap might still have allowed someone to squeeze inside, but the blocking post effectively prevented anyone standing outside being able to see in.

Here was a mystery to ponder later.

A final surprise at this stage was the number and diversity of axe-marks preserved on the timbers. If this really was an Early Bronze Age timber circle, then these were the oldest Bronze Age axe-marks in Britain, made at a time when bronze tools were still supposedly scarce. One theory holds that the introduction of bronze to Britain had initially been resisted by a religious elite – if true, this would have slowed the spread of bronze tools even more. The curvature and width of the axe-marks had not yet been studied in detail, but it looked as though many axes, possibly dozens, had been used to build the Holme timber circle. Nobody had expected that.

Muddy, flat and criss-crossed by streams: a typical north Norfolk saltmarsh today, similar to the environment at Holme-next-the-Sea 4,000 years ago.

The verdict of the court

In the High Court on Tuesday 6 July, the judge who was originally to have heard the case stood down, as he was a member of English Heritage. The case would now be heard by Mrs Justice Arden.

Although the injunctions against Des Crow, Rollo Maughfling, Buster Nolan and 'John Doe' were straightforward in legal terms, the injunction against Geoff Needham was potentially much more interesting. In 1967 he had registered as a common rights holder over land that included Holme beach – he and 183 other local people were entitled to graze livestock on the common land, and to collect various plants, shellfish, game, sand and shingle. They were also entitled to 'estovers', or old timbers, found on the common. Was the Holme timber circle 'estovers'? Possibly – if it was not declared a national monument.

Geoff Needham, however, had neither the time nor the resources to explore this murky and ancient area of English law. Instead, he and his fellow protesters heard the case against them presented by a barrister representing English Heritage, and offered their own defences. Geoff Needham's defence was simple: as a common rights holder he was entitled to be on the beach and, in any case, he had done nothing to obstruct the excavation.

In the event, the injunctions against Geoff Needham and Rollo Maughfling were not upheld. Neither man had attempted to obstruct the archaeologists' work,

Buster Nolan on the steps of the Royal Courts of Justice.

(Below, from left to right) David Gurney, Norfolk's Principal Landscape Archaeologist, Geoff Needham, Chairman of Holme-next-the-Sea Parish Council, and Brian Ayers, County Archaeologist for Norfolk, at a public meeting.

THE MEANING OF METAL

In the Early Bronze Age, metal artefacts and the metalworking skills to produce them were still relatively rare. Tools such as bronze axes and blades had been introduced from the continent, where copper and bronze were already well established, but in Britain their flint and antler counterparts were still very much in use. Later in the Bronze Age an extraordinary range of metal objects was in use – tools alone included awls, chisels, gouges, hammers, punches, sickles and, of course, axes – but earlier, some 4,000 years ago, the rarity of metal objects meant that they were more than mere functional objects. Many discoveries show that Early Bronze Age metal artefacts had a special, symbolic quality.

One way to share in this 'specialness' was to wear it. Personal adornment was already common in the Neolithic Period, with beads, tusks, pins and polished stone all featuring – so metal was a natural addition.

It was also a stark contrast to the stone, pottery and wooden objects of everyday life. There almost certainly was not enough bronze and gold in circulation yet for everyone to wear them freely, however, so metal jewellery and ornaments probably played a significant role in the public, ceremonial side of life. Polished metal adornments might simply have marked a person's status in the social hierarchy, but might also have reflected the growth of individuality. There is also a theory that the introduction of bronze was resisted in Britain by a conservative elite whose supremacy was threatened by the new materials and a new symbolism, in which case the wearing of bronze jewellery would have represented a challenge to authority.

Functionally, bronze tools were (or, early on, were perceived to be) a big advance on flint and other stones, and it is very likely that they conferred status

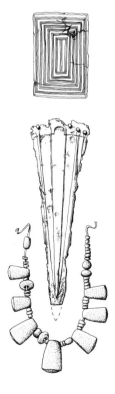

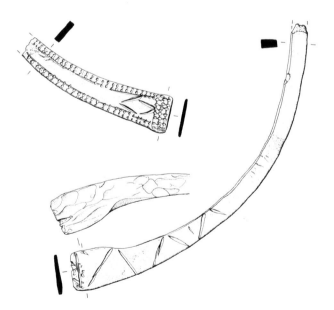

(Left) Early Bronze Age grave goods from a male burial at Little Cressingham in Norfolk: a gold decorative plaque, a bronze dagger and an amber bead necklace.

(Above) Two Bronze Age necklaces from Barton Bendish, Norfolk

on their owners. The key object was the axe. In Neolithic times, the axe had already assumed symbolic importance – beautifully finished jadeite and stone axe heads that were clearly decorative rather than practical have been found in Britain. The tradition continued throughout the Bronze Age, with many axe heads finely polished and ornamented, even on surfaces that would have been hidden when the axe head was attached to its handle.

Bronze objects were also connected with beliefs and mythology. They have often been found in funerary deposits, perhaps connected with the dead person's journey to the next world, but also alone and with other objects in places that were likely locations for ritual and rite-of-passage activities.

Finally, the coming of metal meant more effective weapons. An ornamented dagger was an impressive sign of wealth and status, but a metal cutting edge was a way to inflict damage as never before. As J Cope says in *The Modern Antiquarian*, '[T]he

discovery of metal ... was the first moment when great physical power alone could guarantee a person's place in the community – and that person was almost certain to have always been male. But, most importantly, the arrival of metal meant a severe shift in the possibilities of what violence could achieve. Whereas in the Neolithic period a successful stabbing would have been a considerable achievement, with the coming of bronze weapons bodies could be ripped asunder, limbs hacked off and enemies decapitated.' The change, however, was a gradual one – other than daggers and axes, few metal weapons have been found that date back to the Early Bronze Age, when the Holme timber circle was built.

The assimilation into everyday life of metal ornaments, utensils, tools and weapons did not happen overnight. Rather, over many hundreds of years, metal objects had a profound, transformative effect on the lives of Bronze Age Britons.

(Left) A bronze dagger with replica haft.   *(Above) Polished flint axe heads.*

Mrs Justice Arden ruled, and both were awarded their costs against English Heritage. The injunctions against Des Crow, Buster Nolan and 'John Doe', however, were upheld. Although the judge had some sharp things to say about the 'provocative' actions of English Heritage during the excavation, the outcome was a clear one. Now neither of the two longtime protesters, nor any other member of the public with similar intentions, could interrupt the raising of the Holme timber circle.

High drama: the central oak is lifted

A few days later the excavation was under way again. The team concentrated at first on lifting more of the timbers from the circle, but Mark Brennand and Bill Boismier were keen to remove the central tree sooner rather than later, and there was now plenty of room for a heavy-duty digger to come very close in without damaging any timbers. The tide tables showed that Thursday 15 and Friday 16 July would give the

(Above) After weeks of excavation, protests and courtroom arguments, it was finally time to lift the central oak tree.

(Opposite) Spectators watch, as the digger carries the central oak slowly along the beach, escorted by archaeologists and the police.

The home straight: the final five timbers, still in place at the end of July 1999.

(Below) We did it! The Norfolk Archaeological Unit team, after the lifting of the final timber. From left to right: Simon Underdown, Neil Moss, Fran Green, David Adams, Mark Brennand, Helen Evans, Duncan Stirk, Steve Hickling (crouching), Maisie Taylor and Barry Martin. Team member Pete Warsop is not pictured.

archaeologists the maximum window of opportunity; the two men opted for the Thursday.

The protests had tailed off, so everyone involved in the excavation hoped that the lifting of the central tree would go ahead without a hitch. The day before the planned operation, however, the media had been informed and, not surprisingly, word swiftly reached the protesters, who turned out in numbers. Still, as the tide retreated on the Thursday the central tree was prepared for lifting – heavy foam pads were placed under the slings and chains that would be used to lift it and more sand was scraped away from the base.

Then, just as the diggers were taking up their final positions, the saga of the timber circle took a new twist. Mervyn Lambert, the plant-hire businessman who had underwritten the protesters' legal bills and who was present on the beach, called the Health and Safety Executive to complain that the diggers the archaeologists were about to use to lift the tree were too small to do the job safely.

Mark Brennand conferred with Bryn Williams, the operator of the main digger – unsure of their ground, they decided to bring in a bigger machine just in case. But that would take time, and there was no delaying the tide. The central tree would have one more night on the beach.

The next day the archaeologists arrived early, roped the site off and set about preparing the central tree again. As ever, the media, the police and a host of onlookers were present, together with a few protesters. Soon Bryn Williams approached along the beach from the west, this time with a dumper truck and a twenty-ton tracked excavator. Once the excavator was in position, the slings were attached and the lifting began.

For the casual spectator, this was an interesting moment and a good photo-opportunity, but for the archaeologists it was almost unbearable. 'My heart was pounding and I felt physically sick,' remembers Fran Green, one of the team from Norfolk Archaeological Unit. At this point, they did not know whether the

tree was hollow or solid, or whether it would survive the stresses and strains of the lifting process without disintegrating. Worse still, the team had to watch Bryn Williams gently rock the tree from side to side in order to break the vacuum-seal holding it in place. But then the base of the tree trunk separated from the mud that had held it for 4,000 years, and the archaeologists could breathe again. The tree was intact. 'My God, the tension,' said Dr Francis Pryor afterwards; 'but in the end I'm delighted, because the thing is now safe.'

Still the excitement was not over. As the tree lifted clear of its hole, a young woman protester had ducked under the rope and was sprinting for the tree. One of the NAU archaeologists stopped her, however, and the police pinned her down, while she and a companion screamed and yelled.

As the hysterics continued and the central tree began its stately progress along the beach towards the flat-bed truck that would take it to Flag Fen, two questions were about to be answered.

First, was the tree hollow or solid? A quick inspection showed that it was solid, so there was no hidden offering or hoard or human remains to investigate.

Second, was there anything in the hole left by the tree? No, there was nothing; or almost nothing – just a fragment of honeysuckle rope stuck in the sticky mud at the side of the hole. The following day the archaeologists concentrated their efforts on the area beneath where the tree stump had been, but all they found was a single hazelnut shell. Not quite what everyone had imagined, but still intriguing.

Once the central tree had been lifted, the protests ended. For two weeks the team worked to lift the remaining timbers, with the last two raised on Sunday 1 August. All that remained was for Mark Brennand to scatter a few 1999 coins in the trench that the North Sea would soon refill with sand. Any future archaeologist would know that this particular site on Holme beach had been well and truly excavated.

TIME TEAM

Soon after the decision had been made to excavate the timber circle, Channel 4 gave the go-ahead for Time Team to shoot a 'Seahenge special' documentary, which was ultimately broadcast over the Christmas/New Year holiday. This was not just a longer-than-usual holiday special, however. It was unusual in two other respects. First, the team, led by Tony Robinson, would take no part in the excavation itself and, second, the hour-long programme would have two distinct parts: the story of the excavation as it progressed on Holme beach, and the building of a full-scale reconstruction of the circle.

On the beach, Time Team cameraman Graham Johnston had full, fly-on-the-wall access to the excavation. Over two-and-a-half months, he documented the sheer hard work and determination of the archaeologists, as well as the activities of the media, the protesters, the police and the public. At Flag Fen, he also captured the exciting discovery by timber expert Maisie Taylor of 4,000-year-old honeysuckle rope, still attached to towing loops cut into the central tree stump.

Away from the beach, the reconstruction was intended to test emerging theories about the construction of the timber circle, and so was to be, in the words of executive producer Tim Taylor, 'as authentic as possible'. Time Team recruited experts in prehistoric woodworking, ropemaking, flint-knapping and bronze casting and, not wanting to disturb a sensitive saltmarsh environment, selected a site in an empty corner of a commercial orchard just outside Holme-next-the-Sea.

The trees came from a managed woodland in Bromley, Kent, which the owners were thinning as part of a plan to restore it to its

Presenter Tony Robinson, in thoughtful mood beside the central oak tree.

medieval conditions. Having checked the curvature and width of axe-marks in the excavated timbers, the team's metalworker cast new bronze axe heads in a packed-sand mould. The axes worked well. Flint specialist Phil Harding had produced an authentic stone axe, too, so the tree-fellers could compare the two prehistoric technologies – although the cutting edges of the bronze axes were a little soft (they could have been hardened by further hammering) they still outperformed the flint. The toughest task, though, was getting the stump of the central oak out of the ground. Having felled the tree, whose trunk would provide timbers for the circular wall, the team spent a day and a half trying to grub up the stump... and failed. In the end a tractor wrenched it free. The conclusion was that the Bronze Age woodworkers had probably loosened the tree first by pulling on ropes to rock it to and fro.

Back at Holme, the team dug the central hole and a circular trench with dimensions exactly matching the real timber circle. The oak tree trunks were split by hammering in wooden wedges, and the posts were matched against one another for 'best fit'. Now came perhaps the biggest challenge of all: hauling and erecting the inverted central oak stump.

While woodworker Damien Goodburn stripped the bark from the trunk with a replica Bronze Age adze, rope expert Damien Saunders finished preparing his experimental honeysuckle rope. He had twisted together three honeysuckle stems and found that soaking the rope in water would keep it supple and strong for up to three weeks. The rope was threaded

Using home-made honeysuckle rope, the Time Team crew pulls the central oak towards its position at the centre of the reconstructed timber circle.

Did the Bronze Age circle look like this? After days of hard labour, the Time Team archaeologists, film crew and volunteers survey the finished reconstruction.

through tow-holes cut into the trunk, as on the excavated oak, and a path of rollers was laid for the tree's 25 m (c 82 ft) journey. At the first pull, however, the rope snapped. It was simply not strong enough to withstand a sudden, powerful jerk. Saunders conjured an ingenious 'honeysuckle splice', and the team took the strain again and slowly eased the tree into motion across the rollers. This time ... successfully! In a couple of minutes, six 'pullers' and several 'pushers' moved the one-and-a-half ton oak stump into position.

With no more ado, the stump was levered into the central hole, and propped upright while the team shovelled earth around it. Next, the split timbers were laid out around the trench and erected one by one. Several hours later, Holme-next-the-Sea had its second timber circle, more than 4,000 years after the completion of the first.

In building the reconstruction, the Time Team had learned a great deal about Bronze Age woodworking and ropemaking techniques, but now it was time to stand back and consider the result of their labours. On the outside of the monument, the bark of the split timbers blended naturally with the surroundings, while inside, the freshly split inner wood and the upturned tree created a very private space that felt somehow purified and peaceful. Would the roots of the ancient, upturned tree have held a corpse? It is impossible to know for sure.

'Whatever it was for,' concluded presenter Tony Robinson, 'it still has an enormous sense of power and mystery about it ... You know that feeling you get when you go into a dark and empty church and there's no one around? I don't know what that feeling's about, but that's what you get here.'

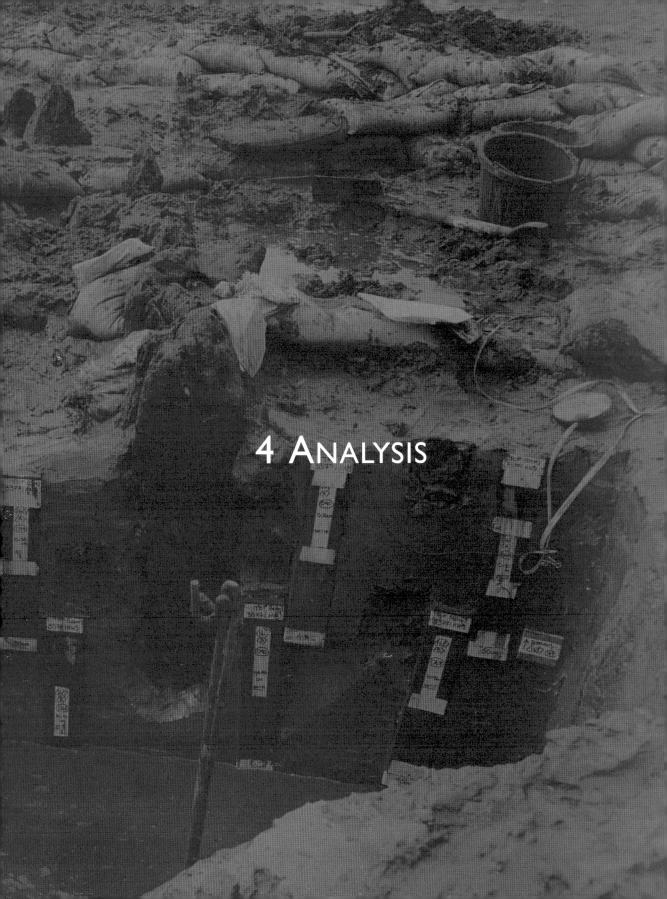

4 ANALYSIS

The Holme timbers at Flag Fen

Flag Fen is a unique Later Bronze Age archaeological site in the Cambridgeshire fens to the east of Peterborough. In 1982 a 'dragline' (a mechanical digger adapted for cleaning out the fenland drainage dykes) unearthed an ancient piece of timber that was subsequently radiocarbon dated to 1000 BC. Since then, excavations have revealed a ritual landscape that includes a timber alignment more than one kilometre long, consisting of more than 60,000 posts. The five rows of posts in the alignment were built and in use between 1350 BC and 950 BC, and around them was a colossal timber platform the size of a football stadium. On the southern side of the timber palisade hundreds of bronze artefacts have been found,

ranging from swords, rapiers and daggers to spearheads, ornamental pins and part of a shield.

Today excavation and study of the site continue, several reconstructions of Bronze Age and Iron Age roundhouses have been built, and a museum and a heritage centre have been opened.

Flag Fen also has excellent facilities for the cleaning and study of ancient timber. There was no better choice as the first stop for the timbers from Holme beach.

When the Holme timbers arrived, just hours after having been lifted, they were taken straight to

Archaeologist Francis Pryor at Flag Fen with the central oak stump from the timber circle.

(Above) *Still on its canvas stretcher, one of the timbers from Holme beach arrives at the Flag Fen Bronze Age centre.*

In the eerie setting of Flag Fen's Hudson Barn, the central oak tree spends its first night away from Holme beach for more than 4,000 years.

Hudson Barn, a building recently donated to Flag Fen in which the staff had built tanks just deep enough to hold the timbers fully submerged in fresh water. The central tree was put into a deeper tank, also filled with fresh water, with a constant light spray directed over it.

Normally, for waterlogged wood excavated from a fresh-water environment, the cleaning process would begin immediately. The Holme timbers, however, had spent 4,000 years in a saltwater environment, which unexpectedly made the initial cleaning easier. 'The timbers weren't cleaned or dried on Holme beach,' says Maisie Taylor, who with Francis Pryor co-founded the Fenland Archaeological Trust, which runs the Flag Fen field centre, 'but simply laid on a foam mattress in a

(Above) Maisie Taylor, co-founder of the Bronze Age centre at Flag Fen, and a leading expert on prehistoric wood.

(Left) Alistair Carty of Archaeoptics and the laser-scanning equipment used to create images of the cleaned timbers.

59

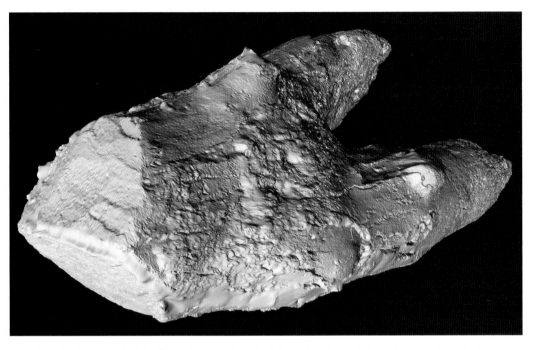

Three-dimensional image of the forked Timber 35/37, produced by Archaeoptics using revolutionary laser-scanning technology.

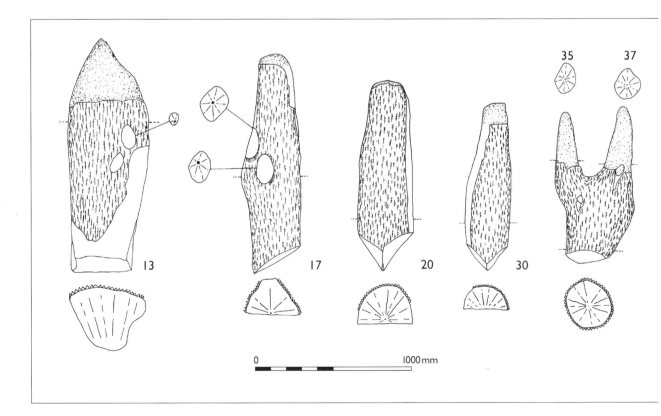

13   17   20   30   35   37

0   1000 mm

trailer and taken to Flag Fen the same day they were lifted. At Flag Fen, they went straight into the fresh water. We found that the salty marine clay that coated the timbers tended to flocculate [that is, it formed small, soft clumps and dropped off].'

Once the delicate job of cleaning had been completed by Flag Fen's enthusiastic staff of students and volunteers, and the timbers had been transferred into long-term holding tanks, the serious interpretive work could begin. This meant examining the timbers visually, noting their dimensions and growth characteristics (straightness and number of branches, for example), and studying the axe-marks left by the prehistoric people who had built the circle.

This analysis, however, was not only visual. Soon after Maisie Taylor had finished her examination of the timbers, a man named Alistair Carty got in touch, offering to use a new, laser-scanning technology to make an accurate 3-D record of the timbers. 'His claims were very impressive,' recalls Maisie Taylor, 'so

English Heritage decided to commission some test scans.' Alistair Carty's new technique easily lived up to its advance billing. The scans produced black-and-white images that show every tiny wrinkle and bulge in the surface of the timbers, and the system allows the operator to manipulate and rotate the image once it has been completed in all dimensions. In effect, it enables achaeologists to reconstruct a virtual model of whatever it is they have excavated. English Heritage quickly commissioned Carty's company, Archaeoptics, to make a full record of all timbers.

Detective work: following Bronze Age clues

Having examined and documented the timbers in minute detail, the next step was to piece the information together to learn as much as possible about the construction of the monument. In a way, it was like modern detective work, only the clues were

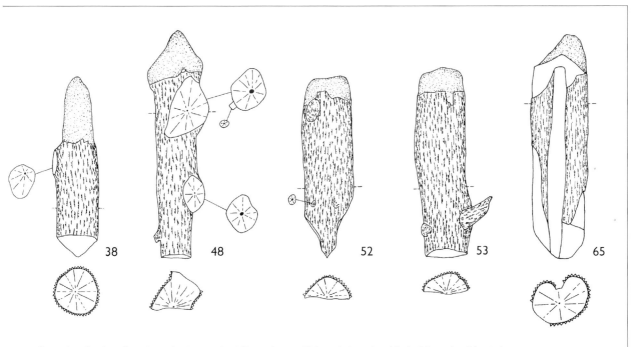

Examples of timbers from the circle, showing the different shaping (V-shaped, slanted and flat) of the ends of the timbers embedded in the earth.

4,000 years old and the people who left them – and the world of the people who left them – were long gone. The ultimate purpose of this highly skilled detective work was to deduce the purpose and meaning of the timber circle, and to increase our knowledge and undertanding of life in Britain during the Early Bronze Age. First, however, the archaeologists had to reconstruct in their minds the scene on the saltmarsh at Holme as the circle was built.

By now Peter Murphy, the English Heritage adviser for archaeological science for eastern England, had progressed in his understanding of the prehistoric environment of the Holme beach site. The evidence suggested, as he believed earlier, that the timber circle was built on a saltmarsh protected from the open sea by a barrier of sand and gravel – a wet environment with a high water table. It is unlikely that anyone lived there permanently; but it is easy to see how this remote, between-dry-land-and-sea quality made it an attractive place to build a monument of special, perhaps religious, significance.

The high water table might also have meant that when the timbers were put into the ground, the construction trench was full of water, before it was back-filled with the sticky, grey saltmarsh mud. The sodden ground was a key factor in the preservation of the timbers. Over time the offshore barrier grew, keeping the sea at bay, and the saltmarsh was gradually transformed into a freshwater wetland. With this change, alder trees colonised the area and a layer of peat began to form on top of the mudflats. Then, as this process continued, sea levels began to rise and the offshore barrier was more frequently breached – over time a cycle developed in which a breached barrier would disappear and a new barrier would form farther inland. As the sea advanced the vegetation disappeared and the layer of peat was covered by sand. In the final years of the 20th century, as the sea level continued to rise, the tides finally washed away much of the sand covering the peat and began to erode the fragile layer of peat itself. This is how, in 1998, the timber circle reappeared.

How did the timber circle, however, fit into this picture of the evolving landscape?

By the late summer of 1999, the timbers had been accurately dated. First, dendrochronologist Cathy Groves had examined the trees' growth rings (see 'A question of age' on page 68 for more details on the science of dating) to produce three possible dates for the felling of the trees: 2454 BC, 2049 BC and 2019 BC. At first, they believed that the central tree had been felled a year earlier than the other trees used by the builders of the circle, but later analysis showed that the sample from the central tree had been taken very close to the root buttressing, where distortion of growth rings is possible, and that two narrow and indistinct rings for the years 2055 BC and 2056 BC had been counted as one.

So the central tree had been felled at the same time as the other trees.

Further, the condition of the sapwood immediately beneath the trees' bark showed that they had been felled during spring or early summer, and the sequence of rings in the trees' last years of life showed that they were growing very slowly, probably owing to increasingly wet conditions. The trees, whose ring sequences were so alike that they almost certainly came from a common woodland source, seem to have been dying.

Radiocarbon analysis – that is, measuring the age of the carbon-14 in samples of organic matter – was also inconclusive, producing a possible date range for the timbers of 2200 BC to 2000 BC. A statistical technique first proposed in 1763 came to the rescue, however. Using Bayesian estimation, named after mathematician and clergyman Thomas Bayes, the team led by Dr Alex Bayliss of English Heritage was able to combine the dendrochronological and radiocarbon dating possibilities to produce a single, conclusive date: 2049 BC.

Confirming that all the trees had been felled at the same time suggested strongly that the building of the circle was a single event. Further, a great amount of work would have been involved in felling, transporting, preparing and erecting the timbers, so it was likely too that the job was done by a large number of people – possibly an entire community or an extended family – working together.

Studying the timbers themselves added weight to this idea of a communal project. The clearest evidence was the axe-marks still visible on many of the timbers – there were dozens of marks, or 'facets', on the lowest parts of the wood, some from felling, others from the trimming of branches, and still more from the cutting of tow-holes in the central tree. Altogether, the toolmarks form probably the largest group of Bronze Age axe-marks yet found in Britain.

The extraordinary preservation of the timber meant that it was possible to measure the width and curvature of each axe blade, and the laser scanning performed by Archaeoptics revealed each axe-mark clearly for posterity. These 'signatures' of the blades could then be compared, and ideas developed about the number of axes used and the number of people using them. The results were a huge surprise to everyone involved. 'Eighteen toolmarks [the marks of 18 different axes] were recorded from the felled tree ends, 23 from the other ends and 10 from trimming up side branches,' wrote Mark Brennand and Maisie Taylor in their report, published in the *Proceedings of the Prehistoric Society*. 'Two other toolmarks were recorded from trimming in slots, four from debris and two from the central tree. This gives a total of 59 possible tools. This total does not, of course, allow for axes cast from identical moulds. Some of the marks are so closely similar that they may possibly have been produced by the same axe. Making allowances for such confusion, the maximum number of tools recorded as being used on this monument is probably nearer 51... The axes may have been resharpened during the construction but, once the blade is set, resharpening should only affect the edges of the blade and should not alter the curvature ratio.'

The discovery that more than 50 bronze axes had been used to build the timber circle – there was no indication that any flint axes had been used – was something of a shock. The monument had been dated to a time when bronze was still thought to be relatively rare, and, some have suggested, only in the hands of a few rich and powerful individuals. What, however, did the number-of-axes revelation imply for the number of people involved? Was the woodworking done by a few individuals with a large stock of axes, much as modern joiners use multiple tools for their work? That possibility cannot be ruled out, but Mark Brennand and Maisie Taylor's knowledge of the Early Bronze Age led them to think otherwise.

It is likely, they wrote, that 'each individual owned the axe that they used. It can be seen that in general the larger axes are used for the felling of the trees and the smaller ones for trimming, but this is not always the case, and smaller axes are used to fell some of the trees. This suggests that it was the individual that was chosen for a particular task, rather than an axe. This figure [a minimum of 51 axes] also suggests that the distribution and ownership of metal axes was widespread at this time, only a few centuries after their introduction.'

The axe-marks left in the timbers were not the only evidence of the way the Early Bronze Age builders

Analysis of the beautifully-preserved axe-marks on the timbers showed that more than 50 individual axes were used in the construction of the Holme timber circle.

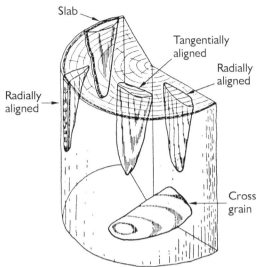

Woodworking debris found during the excavation.

The classification of timber debris.

went about their work. The team also excavated and analysed 422 small pieces of loose wood and bark, the majority of which took the form of woodchips. Much of the bark found was probably attached to the timbers originally, and only one piece of bark bore a chop mark, strongly suggesting that the stripping of bark from the central tree was done before the tree was transported.

The debris contained no leaves or twigs, and almost no 'small roundwood' or side branches, again suggesting that the trimming was done where the trees were felled, rather than at the construction site.

The woodchips themselves were mostly aligned with the grain – the sort of chips that would have been produced while the builders were splitting timbers and

A Bronze Age axe head being comparedto an axe-mark in one of the timbers.

The V-shaped felled end of Timber 30.

The flattened end of Timber 32.

then squaring them up lengthwise to fit snugly against one another in the construction trench. The presence of only a small number of cross-grain woodchips indicates that the squaring-off of timber ends, like the trimming of side branches, was carried out elsewhere, probably as soon as each tree had been felled and quite possibly by people other than those who had felled it.

'The 15–20 trees utilised in the construction of the circle were probably felled by people working in pairs, chopping from opposite sides,' say Brennand and Taylor in their report. 'Each pair felled one, or occasionally two, trees. A further 23 people cut the tops of the trees square. There was no sign of brash [leaves and the smallest twigs], twigs, small or even medium roundwood amongst the debris from the site and it seems probable that the trees were trimmed down to bare trunks before being dragged to the construction site. A further 10 individuals were trimming branches, sometimes working on more than one tree. This might suggest a division of labour, with perhaps the younger or weaker undertaking the lighter tasks. It might even suggest a pattern of small family groups each contributing a small part towards the whole.'

As the archaeologists continued to work on the

clues left by the builders of the Holme timber circle, the picture they were building of the construction site was becoming clearer. Other aspects of the timbers added further detail.

One curious discovery was that while some of the timber-ends set in the ground had classic V-shaped felled ends (where the point of the V is the 'hinge' left after felling a tree by cutting it on both sides), others had flattened ends or ends trimmed on a slant. There is no clear reason for choosing a slanted end rather than a blunt, squared-off end, but the relatively low number of V-shaped ends (16 timbers out of 55) suggests that many of the timbers were cut from the same trees, each trunk providing four or more split posts. If the posts really were three metres in length, they might have come from trees whose usable trunks were at least six metres long. This idea is given further credibility by the dendrochronological analysis, which showed that the central trunk and the 55 circle-timbers came from no more than 15 or 20 individual trees.

The two tow-holes cut into the trunk of the central tree, together with clear wear on one side of it, made it obvious that the tree had been dragged into position. Most fascinating of all, though, was the sophisticated rope the ancient builders had used,

which was made from honeysuckle stems. Honeysuckle rope had never been encountered before, but there was enough preserved at Holme for the archaeologists to learn a good deal.

The rope was made from three roundwood stems (ie whole and unseparated along their lengths), between 15mm and 22mm in diameter. Each stem had been twisted in a clockwise direction – going against honeysuckle's natural tendency to curl anticlockwise – tearing the stems open and making them more pliable; the three stems had then been plied together in an anticlockwise direction, this time working with the plant's natural twining. Once the rope was ready for use, it had been looped around the stripped trunk, passing through both tow holes, and knotted. When the builders tipped the central tree into its hole, the rope was still tied around the trunk, and was trapped and abandoned.

After the central tree had been lifted in July 1999, the 4,000-year-old honeysuckle knot was found *in situ*, stuck to the mud at the side of the hole. More honeysuckle rope was found, still within the tow holes, by Maisie Taylor when she was examining the stump at Flag Fen. The lessons learned from the preserved rope were invaluable for the Time Team reconstruction of the timber circle [see page 54] and, in turn, the practical experience gained by ropemaker Damien Saunders added to the archaeologists' understanding of honeysuckle as a raw material.

As well as the wood and honeysuckle rope fragments and the axe-marks left on the timbers, the way the timbers had been placed led Mark Brennand and Maisie Taylor to develop a persuasive theory about the sequence of construction. They thought they could detect two distinctive 'panels' of posts within the circle, made up of sequences of adjacent timbers, in the south-west and north-east quadrants. In the south-west panel were four of the five roundwood timbers in the circle and, at the centre of the panel, the forked

timber, which might have been an entrance.

Facing the forked timber, at the centre of the north-east panel, was the fifth roundwood timber, flanked on either side by a small half-split timber and several large timbers that had been further trimmed after splitting. Four of these large, unusually split timbers came from the same tree as the central stump. The remaining two arcs of the circle were made up exclusively of half-split timbers set edge to edge – 20 in the south-east arc and 18 in the north-west – all but one of which had been placed with their bark facing outward and the split surface inward.

The south-west to north-east alignment of the central timbers in the two panels suggested a celestial

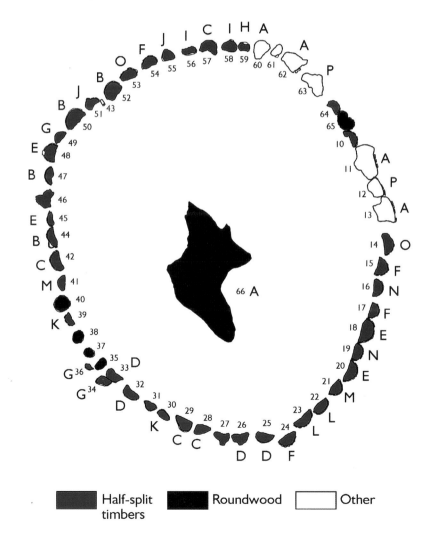

The location of the roundwood, half-split and other split timbers within the circle, and the individual trees (lettered) from which the timbers were cut.

Half-split timbers   Roundwood   Other

A QUESTION OF AGE

The scientific approach to dating historic artefacts and organic materials has revolutionised archaeology. In the 1960s, by which time radiocarbon dating had been accepted as reliable, archaeologists were having to abandon long-established ideas about the dates and durations of prehistoric periods – the Neolithic and Bronze Ages, for example, which were previously imagined as much briefer than we now know they were – and to rethink the way they approached their work. Today, the science of dating ancient objects is an integral part of archaeology.

In the dating of the Holme timber circle, three techniques were combined to give an exceptionally precise date for the felling of the oak trees.

The first was dendrochronology, the study of growth rings in trees. The number of rings gives the age of a tree and, as the width of each ring reflects the local climatic conditions in that year (a narrow ring in a dry year, a wider one in a wet year), it is possible to compare a sequence of growth rings to the known climatic record. Over time, dendrochronologists have constructed graphs showing climatic fluctuations, season by season in particular regions, that go back thousands of years. Matching the short graph of an individual tree's growth to the long, climatic-record graph (that is, finding a matching sequence of 'wiggles' on the two graphs) gives a probable date when the tree was felled. For the Holme timber circle, this process yielded three possible dates for the central tree: 2454 BC, 2050 BC and 2019 BC.

One extra detail dendrochronologists look for is the size of the pores in the sapwood immediately below the bark, as these vary according to the season. The trees used at

Counting the rings: a polarised light micrograph through the stem of an oak tree.

Holme were felled during spring or early summer.

The second technique is radiocarbon dating, which produces estimated dates by measuring the amounts of carbon-14 in samples of organic matter. Carbon-14 is a radioactive form (or isotope) of carbon released into the earth's atmosphere by the constant bombardment of the earth by sub-atomic particles. Plants absorb it as part of the carbon dioxide they need, and animals then take it in when they eat the leaves. Even carnivorous creatures will acquire carbon-14 from the animals they eat. For dating purposes, however, the essential characteristic of carbon-14 is its uniform rate of decay – the quantity of carbon-14 in a piece of wood, charcoal, fabric or bone will give an accurate estimate of its age.

Lingering uncertainty (caused by fluctuations in cosmic radiation and the often tiny sample sizes available) means that radiocarbon dates are given as a range rather than as a precise date. The wood samples taken at Holme yielded a range of 2200 BC to 2000 BC.

Bayesian estimation was the statistical technique that unified the dendrochronological and radiocarbon analyses to give a single, accurate date. First proposed in a paper published posthumously in 1763 by mathematician and clergyman Thomas Bayes, Bayesian estimation is widely used today and enabled the Holme researchers to combine the two sets of probable dates to produce one extremely narrow range of probability. After further growth-ring analysis had revealed that the second of the three possible dendrochronological dates for the central tree was 2049 BC, rather than 2050 BC, Bayesian estimation revealed that all the timbers used in the Holme timber circle were felled in the spring or early summer of 2049 BC.

orientation, aligning with the midwinter sunset in the south-west and midsummer sunrise in the north-east.

Was the timber circle used for regular observations? It is impossible to know for sure. The size of the gap in the forked timber makes exact sightlines difficult to determine, and the unknown height and distance from the circle of the coastal barrier (between the saltmarsh and the sea) in 2049 BC means that it is impossible to calculate exactly where the rising and setting of the sun and moon would have occurred, as viewed through the forked timber.

Perhaps the midsummer sunrise to midwinter sunset alignment was, however, simply a starting point for the building process, symbolically aligning the structure along the axis of life (midsummer sunrise) and death (midwinter sunset). The archaeologists believe that once the central tree had been set in place, the forked timber and the roundwood timber opposite were aligned and erected, followed by the timbers flanking them in their respective panels. Then, when the two panels were complete, the two arcs of half-split timbers were erected to complete the circle.

Another intriguing possibility connected with the south-west to north-east alignment arose from the archaeologists' records of the depths to which the timbers were set. Towards the south-west the timbers were set more shallowly, and towards the north-east more deeply, than the average depth. If all the timbers were cut to the same length (and there is some suggestion that they might have been, as timbers from a single tree were usually set to the same depth, implying that they were the same length), then the timbers in the north-east panel would have been lower than the timbers in the 'side arcs', and the timbers in the south-west, where the forked entrance was located, would have been higher. In that case, the height of the circle at those two significant points of the compass would have made the monument's alignment very clear indeed.

(Overleaf) An evocative rendition, by artist Judith Dobie, of how midsummer sunrise might have appeared over the newly constructed timber circle.

Archaeologist Fran Green, with soil-sample tins in place around Timber 12.

Environmental analysis: pollen, insects and soil

While Mark Brennand and Maisie Taylor were focusing on the individual timbers and on the circle as a whole, other specialists had begun to conduct laboratory analysis of the many soil samples taken during the excavation. The primary goal was to prove whether or not the timbers making up the circle had been inserted into a 'construction cut' (a prepared trench). The form of the timbers and the discovery of woodworking debris strongly suggested that they had, but the archaeologists wanted to be certain; they wanted to learn as much as possible about the building techniques of the Early Bronze Age.

The forensic element of the detective work had begun.

The first step was to analyse the sediment itself. When the radial trenches were cut, ready for the archaeologists to take samples before lifting the timbers, they often exposed what appeared to be a cross-section of the expected construction trench: while the undisturbed sediment was a dark blue-grey, the supposedly back-filled soil packed around the timbers was lighter in colour. Surely this visual evidence was proof enough of the construction-cut theory?

Sadly not. The dark greyish tone of the sediments comes from marine organic matter, which changes colour when it comes into contact with oxygen. One possibility is that, over 4,000 years, the timbers themselves had oxidised the sediments nearest to them, causing the colour difference.

Under a microscope, however, there was another difference between samples of soil from undisturbed areas and samples from the possible construction cut: the 'organisation' of the sediment. Essentially, the undisturbed sediments exhibited fine 'micro-layering', which the construction-cut material did not. Digging and then back-filling during the building process could easily have destroyed the layering. Further, some samples were taken in which the 'cut line', or border between undisturbed, micro-layered sediment and the back-fill, was clearly visible when magnified. The case for the construction-cut was getting stronger.

Analysis of plant remains in the samples made the case stronger still. The types of plant matter found confirmed that the timber circle was built in an area of saltmarsh, with some areas of sparsely vegetated mud-flat near by. More telling, though, was the density of material recovered. On average, 1.6 seeds/fruits per litre were recovered from the undisturbed sediments, while 6.13 seeds/fruits per litre were found in the construction cut (and 5.5 in the clay beneath the central tree). The difference between the figures is a clear indication of digging and back-filling.

The insect remains in the samples tell a similar story. Undisturbed samples produced 0.1 items per litre, while construction-cut samples yielded 0.7 items per litre. In general, the community of insects was one associated with saltmarsh and mud-flats, but the remains of several dung beetles raised the possibility that the land was grazed, and several grassland insects were found, consistent with the idea that there might have been grass-covered dunes on the inland side of the saltmarsh.

The most interesting find was a single specimen of *Laemophloeus monilis*, a flattened fungal-feeding beetle that is found beneath the bark of deciduous trees, including oak. Today it is an extremely rare beetle, found in only two places in Britain, both of which contain trees of ancient woodland and pasture woodland. It is likely that *Laemophloeus monilis* arrived on the Holme saltmarsh 4,000 years ago under the bark of one of the trees used for the timber circle, and so also likely that the trees were brought from an area of old woodland or wooded pasture.

Was there such an area close to the saltmarsh? Close examination of the pollen found among the tree samples suggests there might have been. Among the tree pollen recorded, alder (which is well adapted to growing in wet conditions) was common, as expected, but so were oak, pine and lime. 'The general indication therefore,' says the report of the excavation,

(Above) A gnarled, slow-growing oak tree, whose form is a response to wet conditions.

A well-preserved specimen of Laemophloeus monilis, a species of rare, fungal-feeding beetle found during the excavation.

in respect of one particular sample, 'is one of a mixed oak woodland on the dry land that flanks the sample location.'

Another sample, and an intriguing one, came from a fragment of peat found in the back-fill to the now-proven construction cut – the fragment might have been dragged to the site attached to one of the oak trunks. The combination of pollen and amoebas present in the sample pointed to a wet woodland in which alder and hazel would grow well, but oak would struggle. Alder, however, was not as well represented as expected, while oak was strongly represented. One conclusion, which would agree with the tree-ring analysis that suggested that the felled trees were dying, was that the relatively dry oak woodland was becoming wetter as a result of changes in the water table, possibly as a result of a rise in sea level.

From celestial alignment to the Dagenham idol

Having examined the timbers, the builders' methods, the finished structure, the sediments, the insects, the pollen, the plant remains and more besides, the archaeologists were left with one more question to address: why?

In a short period of time in 2049 BC, a community of Early Bronze Age people had decided to fell, trim, transport and prepare between 15 and 20 mature oak trees, which together weighed many tons. Then they turned their hard-won raw material into a timber circle surrounding an upturned oak stump, which alone weighed two tons. The evidence showed, according to Maisie Taylor in the final report, that 'the number of people involved in the felling could be... 50–80,' which 'does not allow for people involved only in tasks that have left no direct evidence: the production of the rope, the towing or dragging of the wood, the splitting of the timbers, the digging of the

Was the central, upturned oak an excarnation platform?
If so, Judith Dobie's illustration shows how the scene might
have looked.

trenches, the erection of the timbers and the supply of food and drink.'

So what was the meaning of the Holme timber circle?

Since the earliest days of the excavation, the most frequently voiced theory has been that the skyward-pointing roots of the central tree formed an excarnation platform, on which a corpse would have been left to be exposed to the elements, so that, as the flesh decomposed (or was even carried away by birds), the soul was released. There is evidence for this practice in British prehistory, and this very credible idea is still the favourite of many archaeologists. The splayed roots looked ready-made to hold something the size of a human body, and the circle itself was neither big enough, nor easy enough to enter, for it to

An imaginative reconstruction of the building process, showing the possible construction sequence: north-east and south-west 'panels' first, then the central oak, and finally the remaining 'side arcs'.

have been used for large group ceremonies. It also had a 'remarkably distinctive, closed architecture' – that is, people outside the circle could not see in – which perhaps echoes the sort of lonely privacy one finds in a chapel of rest today.

Excarnation is not the only possibility, however. Mark Brennand, site manager for the excavation of the circle, wrote in *British Archaeology* magazine in September 2004 that 'Early in the project, when asked by journalists, I simply spieled off theories of excarnation and an inverted underworld. I now feel less inclined to suggest a body was ever laid within the tree roots.' The hardest part of the project, he says in the article, 'was after the excavation: finding a way of interpreting the uninterpretable.'

Right up until the day the central tree was lifted, the archaeologists had expected to discover something buried beneath it that would explain the timber circle's presence. Human remains or personal belongings, for example, would have given the monument a clear logic. The hole left by the tree, however – and the grey sediment beneath and immediately around it – were empty.

Another possibility was that the circle had been filled in, with the edge-to-edge timbers acting as a retaining wall for a mound covering the inverted central tree. Again, though, the evidence did not support the theory. For one thing, there was no sign of any substantial ditch from which infill material would have been quarried. Also, the thin 'blocking post' driven into the ground immediately outside the forked branches of the narrow entrance would have stopped people seeing in, but would not have stopped earth falling out. A forked post would have been a strange component in any sort of retaining wall.

The distinctive appearance of the wall, however, did seem to be significant. All but one of its timbers were positioned with bark facing outwards, giving the circle the look of a giant tree stump. Surely the single timber with its split face to the outside cannot have been a mistake. Only at a single point was the internal wood of the tree exposed. Perhaps it represented a natural phenomenon, possibly a scar on one of the original trees. The roundwood timber directly opposite the forked entrance had a prominent scar, for instance, and the archaeologists believe that one of the trees used might have been struck by lightning. Otherwise, each timber in the circle might represent an individual or group involved in the construction, and the reversed timber might refer symbolically to a particular person. It is even possible that one, several or all of the timbers were carved above ground, making personal symbolism even more likely. The 'Dagenham idol' – a 0.5 m [c 19¾ in] pine figure found in the Thames

Marshes in 1912 and radiocarbon dated to between 2640 BC and 1980 BC – shows that the people of the Early Bronze Age used knives as well as axes, and were capable of intricate carving.

What is certain is that trees had a powerful significance. Not only did trees provide fruit, fuel and building materials to prehistoric people, but they are likely to have been metaphors for life, death and regeneration, and possibly to have held symbolic meanings dependent on their locations, appearances and histories. Trees had been used in the construction of monuments for thousands of years before the Holme timber circle – three massive post-holes near Stonehenge date from the eighth millennium BC, for example – and there are many recorded instances of Neolithic artefacts deposited in 'tree-throws', the hollows left by uprooted trees.

It is even possible that the health of local oak trees was the reason for the construction of the circle. Analysis of the tree rings and pollen samples showed that the trees were under stress owing to wetter climatic conditions, and the squared-off end of the central stump suggested that that tree had not been felled in the normal way, but might have fallen naturally. Was the monument a tree-sacrifice to a natural deity in a bid to save the remaining oak trees? The south-west to north-east alignment of the circle's two most distinctive timbers – the forked entrance and the roundwood timber directly opposite – is suggestive of the opposition of life (midsummer sunrise) and death (midwinter sunset), and the trees' struggle for life and the fertility of the land might have been just as important, or even more so, than the lives and deaths of individual people.

The 'Dagenham idol', a Bronze Age, carved pine figure found in the Thames marshes in 1912.

EARLY BRONZE AGE SYMBOLISM AND ASTRONOMY

The people of the Early Bronze Age left no written record of their way of life, and only a handful of dwellings have survived, so we rely for almost all our knowledge of them on their funerary sites, on hoards and individual finds of bronze and other artefacts, and on their monuments. Even from these few sources, some aspects of the symbolic values of the time are clear.

A common motif is circularity. Barrows, ring-ditches and henges are all round, often involving concentric circles, and usually have objects or burials in their centres. This roundness echoes many aspects of the natural world, from the shape of the sun and moon to the roundness of tree trunks, as in the Holme timber circle.

Also connected with death and the transition to the next life in another world is inversion. Ceramic pots have been found inverted in many Bronze Age burial sites, often containing cremated human remains – the inversion of the pot is suggested to be symbolic of the life-to-death transformation. The exact meaning of inverted trees and timbers is not fully understood, but trees have a central role in many ancient cultures, representing life and, in some cases, a connection with the world beneath. Inverting a tree might have been a way of making an offering to a deity, or a way of transforming an everyday-but-valuable part of life into something sacred.

The practice of making offerings, of pleasing ancestors or deities, was not limited to burial and monument sites. Many hundreds of precious and/or practical objects – from swords and dress pins to bracelets and buttons – have been found, sometimes alone and sometimes as part of a hoard, in situations that make it clear that they were placed deliberately and not simply lost or abandoned.

Finally, in some cases there seem to have been astronomical connections in many Early Bronze Age monuments. There has been great controversy over Stonehenge, for example: some archaeologists have claimed that it is a complex observatory and that its builders had advanced knowledge of celestial movements. However advanced Stonehenge may be, there is no doubt that some monuments of the period were built deliberately along celestial alignments. The sun and moon were clearly important, and midsummer and midwinter were probably very significant dates in the Early Bronze Age calendar.

Stonehenge: an observatory, a ceremonial arena... or both?

The world turned upside down

Central to any interpretation of the Holme timber circle is the great upturned oak stump inside it. Why did the builders of the circle invert the central tree?

Many cultures around the world had, and some still have, beliefs about various aspects or stages of life and the afterlife taking place below, on and above the earth. Other excavations have shown that during the Early and Middle Bronze Ages there were connections between death and inversion. At Holme, the inversion of the tree might have been symbolic of the end of a life, the offering of life to the earth or to the next world, or the transformation of the tree from the world of the living into the world of the dead. In his book *Seahenge*, Francis Pryor makes the point that the trees were felled during spring or early summer, the season of new growth, when their life forces were at their most vigorous. 'The mighty [inverted] oak perhaps symbolises life itself – the Tree of Life of

The inverted central oak stump in situ. Was it meant to penetrate or signify another world?

Time Team presenter Tony Robinson: 'Whatever it was for, it still has an enormous sense of power and mystery about it.'

medieval mythology,' he writes. 'So a living organism of this world is being offered to the world below the ground, which was possibly seen as the source of all life. It's about propitiation and renewal. It's also about the cycle of life and indeed the cycle of the seasons.'

There is evidence, too, that the Holme timber circle was built within, and as part of, a 'special' area of the landscape, where religious activity was concentrated. It was situated on marshy, probably uninhabitable land on the edge of the world of the Early Bronze Age people – that is, by the sea, which was seen in some cultures as the realm of the ancestors – and it is not the only ritual discovery to have been made.

The most significant find was another, larger timber circle – named 'Holme II' by the archaeologists – about 100m east of the excavated circle. Although it had not been excavated, Holme II appeared to be made from split planks set edge to edge, and had two large, parallel oak logs at its centre, set within an oak-hurdle-lined pit. Each log had a rounded 'scoop' carved out of its top by an axe, perhaps to create a platform for a coffin or bier (a frame on which a body is placed). It is possible that the pit was covered by an earthen mound, a common burial practice in the east of Britain and on the continent at the time. Radiocarbon dating suggests that the Holme II circle was built several centuries earlier (2400–2030 BC) than the excavated circle, but it would have been visible when the smaller circle was under construction and the two monuments might have been in use at the same time.

Other finds that suggest the Bronze Age saltmarsh might have been a 'ritual' landscape include a number of bronze objects discovered on the beach and a possible trackway made up of 52 lengths of parallel horizontal wood. There are other round barrows in the area, too, including a group of four ploughed-out ring-ditches 2.5km south of Holme beach.

In addition, 3km west of Holme, in a former saltmarsh landscape just like the one on which the timber circle was built, in 1974 a landowner discovered a Bronze Age hoard that included an axe head, a bracelet, two neck-rings and a dress pin. Such a collection of valuable items was almost certainly deposited in the uninhabitable swamp as an offering to the gods or the ancestors.

There was no hoard under the Holme timber circle, nor was it a typical burial barrow. Also, while it was roughly circular, the monument's structure and appearance were strikingly different from those of other Early Bronze Age wooden monuments. The archaeological investigation revealed lots of remarkable detail about the building process, however, and perhaps there are more answers to be found here.

The Holme circle was the result of a community joining together at a single time to create a single structure – the building of the circle was an 'event'. 'It may have marked the death of an individual, the death of a tree, or the regenerative failure of the trees,' wrote Mark Brennand and Maisie Taylor. 'It may have commemorated a past event or life and equally it may have represented the culmination of an annual celebration or festival.' We can never know for sure.

What is certain, however, the report continues, is that 'the arrangement and use of timber, trees and tree parts conceals a complex network of symbols. While the trees were split and cut to length the external appearance of the trees was retained and re-emphasised. The exterior of the circle presented a living, natural facade of oak bark while, hidden within the interior, the huge oak was turned on its head, removed from the world of the living but perhaps penetrating into or signifying another.'

The tree-ring and woodworking analyses show that the Holme timber circle was made in an intense burst of communal activity in the spring or early summer of 2049 BC, and then, quite possibly, never re-entered. Perhaps the building of the circle – that intense burst of communal energy, rather than the end result – was the whole point.

An axe head, two neck-rings and a dress pin from the 'Hunstanton hoard', discovered 3km west of Holme-next-the-Sea in 1974.

0   25mm

5 PRESERVATION...
AND THE FUTURE

Bringing the circle home to Norfolk

At Flag Fen the Holme timbers were cleaned, studied and thoroughly documented. The tanks there, however, were only a temporary stop. For a short period the wood could be kept stable in the storage tanks, but if the next phase in the preservation process did not begin soon, the timbers would start to deteriorate. The problem was, only a handful of universities and archaeological trusts in Britain are equipped to carry out specialist preservation work on ancient timber. Also, the work takes time, so there is always a backlog of timbers from sites around the UK waiting their turn to be preserved.

Soon, though, English Heritage had reached agreement with the Mary Rose Trust to process the timbers of the Holme circle. The Trust was originally formed to conserve the wood of the Mary Rose, the Tudor warship raised from the seabed of the Solent. The work on the Mary Rose itself continues, but the Trust has sufficient capacity (not to mention the need to generate an income) to take on other projects, such as the Holme timber circle. It was also one of only two timber-preservation centres with facilities large enough to deal with the Holme circle's great oak stump.

The archaeologists believed that when the circle was built, the groundwater table was not far below the surface, so the timbers were immediately plunged into water. The fact that they were constantly wet and in an oxygen-free (anaerobic) environment accounts for their excellent state of preservation. What had changed during the circle's 4,000-year stay on Holme beach, however, was the make-up of the wood. Over time, the cellulose that gives plant matter its cell structure, and thus its strength, had decayed and been replaced by a slow accretion of mineral salts from the waterlogged sediments. In effect, these mineral salts were holding the timbers together.

Once the the circle had been excavated, however, if the timbers were to be preserved in the long term, the mineral salts would have to be not only removed, but also replaced by another substance that would maintain the structure and strength of the wood. That substance is wax.

Over a period of years, the timbers will be sprayed continuously with a solution of fresh water and wax. The proportion of wax in the solution is tiny, but as the water gradually washes away the mineral salts, so the

One of the preservation tanks at the Mary Rose Trust, where timbers from the Holme timber circle are being treated.

Prince Charles at the Mary Rose Trust, learning about the conservation of ancient wood.

wax will slowly accumulate and replace them. Ultimately, the wax will reinforce the cell structure of the wood.

The timbers will emerge in batches from this preservation process, as they have been sent at different times from Flag Fen to the Mary Rose Trust, and because the bigger the timber, the longer the process takes. The central tree stump will be the last of the Holme timbers to leave the Mary Rose Trust, probably in 2007.

Their new home will be back in west Norfolk, just a few miles from Holme beach, at the refurbished King's Lynn Museum. Thanks to a funding package worth more than £1 million – mostly from the Heritage Lottery Fund, and with supporting funds from Norfolk County Council – the former Union Baptist Chapel will by 2007 have had its entrance remodelled and 1960s suspended ceilings removed, creating a more open and atmospheric exhibition space. 'The final display will probably be in place some time during 2007,' says Robin Hanley, Area Museums Officer. 'The final design for the

display of the Holme circle has yet to be decided [at the time of writing in 2004], but we will probably display half the timbers, as found, with a screen behind them showing changing views of Holme beach. The timbers will be on open display and not behind glass.'

An artist's impression of the display of the Holme timber circle at the refurbished King's Lynn Museum.

Brian Ayers, County Archaeologist for Norfolk.

The continuing story at Holme-next-the-Sea

Meanwhile, the tides and waves of the North Sea continue their relentless work on Holme beach. In many places the peat layer that protected the timber circle for so long has disappeared, and the beach itself continues to get steeper. Although the 'Holme II' circle 100m east of the excavated circle has been fully investigated and recorded, one of the two timbers at its centre has been washed away (the other was rescued) and the erosion goes on. If the Holme timber circle had not been excavated in 1999, it too would now have gone. The excavation took place just in time.

Since then, a lot has been learned. The exact purpose of the monument and the meaning of the upturned oak stump can never be known for sure, so the Holme timber circle will always be something of an archaeological conundrum. The investigation of the site, however, has made a big contribution to the study of the Early Bronze Age. 'The Holme timber circle has had an enormous impact on our understanding of that period in Norfolk, the UK and on the continent,' says Brian Ayers, County Archaeologist for Norfolk. 'The

(Overleaf) Late afternoon sun produces a beautiful scene during the excavation of the timber circle on Holme beach.

range of preservation is so great, including the circle that was excavated, the Holme II circle and the trackway, that we know a lot more about the creation of monuments, the technicalities of construction and the social organisation of the builders. And we've learned a lot about the nature of preservation itself.

'We've also learned a lot about the nature of archaeology and about the way it's perceived by the public. In Britain, conflict over archaeology is unusual. That's not the case in countries like Israel, Australia and even the US, where there are religious and cultural objections to excavating ancient sites. But here archaeologists are generally seen as environmentalists, often rushing in to save and document as much as possible before the developers move in to put a road or a car park or an office block over a site.

'At Holme, the situation was similar in every way except one. We were dealing with a "change event" where the historic environment was about to be destroyed, and our job was to manage that event and to understand, as best we could, what would otherwise have been lost. The difference in this case was that the agent of change wasn't a developer, but the sea, and people perceive the waves very differently from bulldozers. So, for a variety of reasons, we were seen by some as "the experts", "destroying" the historic environment. In future we know we have to proceed more carefully, more openly and to consult with all interested parties. We can't arrest change, but it's essential to get agreement about how we manage it.'

Mapping the landscape, understanding the past

Actively managing — and anticipating — change is becoming a significant aspect of archaeology, and not only in north-west Norfolk. At Holme itself, Norfolk Archaeological Unit has been commissioned to undertake an ongoing 'walkover survey', fully recording the archaeology of the area. This work fits within the context of a broader survey of the north Norfolk coast, being carried out in partnership with English Heritage. The first stage of this survey was desk-based evaluation of coastal records and photography, but important fieldwork is now under way in intertidal areas along one of the world's fastest-changing coastlines.

The coastal survey is linked in turn to the National Mapping Programme, in which archaeologists and other specialists will examine aerial photographs and other existing records to locate, map and record historic sites that might have been missed. The search will take in an enormous quantity of archive material belonging to English Heritage, and will involve the reassessment of thousands of aerial photographs dating from the 1930s to the present day.

A third level of landscape analysis is the Historic Landscape Characterisation Project, which will cover the entire country, assessing the nature and significance of historic landscapes. The starting point for the project is that there is no primeval landscape left — humankind's influence is everywhere, so every landscape is historic.

'The knowledge we will gain from these projects will enable us to "manage" the landscape,' explains Brian Ayers, 'and to understand it more thoroughly, so we know where, when and how to intervene. We want to get away from the "points of history" approach to archaeology. For example, to understand the Holme timber circle properly, you have to link it back to the landscape and the processes of change over the last 4,000 years. Archaeologically, the Norfolk landscape is a very rich one and it continues to surprise us. No one would ever have predicted that we'd find an upstanding timber structure more than 4,000 years old! So who knows what we'll find next, or where we'll find it. In the end, the landscape is so much more complex and more diverse than we can imagine.'

A VERY SENSITIVE ENVIRONMENT

Regular monitoring and recording continues at Holme beach, but even for the trained eye there is very little to see that is of archaeological interest. Further, the ecosystem at the Holme Dunes reserve is an extremely sensitive one – the reserve is a Site of Special Scientific Interest (SSSI), as well as being a wetland of international importance under the Ramsar Convention. Excessive visitor numbers are a threat to the habitat of many birds and other creatures.

The best way to experience the world of the Early Bronze Age is to visit Flag Fen in Cambridgeshire, or to visit the preserved Holme timber circle when it goes on display at the refurbished King's Lynn museum.

Holme Dunes reserve: a rich mix of coastal habitats that include saltmarsh, sand dunes, sand and shingle bars, intertidal sands and mudflats, freshwater and brackish pools, reedbed and grazing marsh.

BIBLIOGRAPHY

Adkins, Lesley and Adkins, Roy 1998 *The Handbook of British Archaeology*. Constable and Robinson

Anonymous 2003 *Where to See Wildlife in Norfolk*. Norfolk Wildlife Trust

Barber, Martyn 2003 *Bronze and the Bronze Age*. Tempus Publishing Limited

Brennand, Mark and Taylor, Maisie 2003 'The Survey and Excavation of a Bronze Age Timber Circle at Holme-next-the-Sea, Norfolk, 1998-9'. *Proceedings of the Prehistoric Society* Vol 69, 1–84

Champion, Matthew 2000 *Seahenge. A Contemporary Chronicle*. Barnwell's Timescape Publishing

Cope, J 1988 *The Modern Antiquarian*. Thorsons

Dymond, David 1985 *The Norfolk Landscape*. Hodder and Stoughton

Glob, P V 1974 *The Mound People. Danish Bronze Age Man Preserved*. Faber and Faber

Parker Pearson, Mike 1999 'The Earlier Bronze Age'. *The Archaeology of Britain*, 77–94. Routledge

Pitts, Mike 2000 *Hengeworld*. Century

Pryor, Francis 2001 *Seahenge. A Quest for Life and Death in Bronze Age Britain*. HarperCollins

Wade-Martins, Peter (ed) 1993 *An Historical Atlas of Norfolk*. Norfolk Museums Service in association with the Federation of Norfolk Historical and Archaeological Organisations

Wade-Martins, Susanna 1984 *A History of Norfolk*. Phillimore and Company

Wymer, J J 1996 'Norfolk and the History of Palaeolithic Archaeology in Britain'. *A Festival of Norfolk Archaeology*, 3–10. The Norfolk and Norwich Archaeological Society

GLOSSARY

barrow a burial mound, usually of earth. Long barrows usually belong to the Neolithic period, and round barrows to the Bronze Age, although some date to the Roman and Anglo-Saxon periods. Early Bronze Age barrow types include bell barrows, disc barrows, pond barrows and saucer barrows.

beaker pottery a type of handleless and highly decorated drinking vessel found in many areas of central and western Europe and characteristic of the late Neolithic and Early Bronze Age.

crop mark a mark or pattern in vegetation that reveals details of buried features, most often revealed in aerial photographs.

dendrochronology a dating method for timber, based on tree-ring sequences.

estovers in full, the legal term is common of estovers, which is the right to take wood for fuel, repairs or other purposes from land one does not own.

Fens, the a flat low-lying area, formerly marshland, covering parts of Cambridgeshire, south Lincolnshire and west Norfolk. Since the 17th century, large parts of the Fens have been drained for agriculture.

Global Positioning System (GPS) a satellite-based technology that enables landscape features to be located with extreme accuracy.

henge a ritual monument, usually circular, consisting of a ditch and, outside it, a bank.

Homo erectus an extinct form of human that lived during the Middle Pleistocene, about half a million years ago.

Homo sapiens 'modern' human, who probably first evolved in Africa around 200,000 years ago.

ice age a period characterised by the expansion of continental and alpine glaciers. Major 'cold stages', or glacials, in Britain include the Anglian, the Wolstonian and, most recently, the Devensian.

interglacial a relatively warm climatic period between glacials (or ice ages).

Mesolithic the 'Middle Stone Age', beginning with the retreat of the glacial ice some time after 9000 BC and ending in Britain with the arrival of Neolithic technology.

Neolithic the period – lasting some 2,500 years in Britain, between the Mesolithic and the Bronze Age – during which people began to use ground stone tools, cultivate plants and keep livestock.

palstave a type of bronze axe in which a ridge separates an open socket from the blade, and flanges on either side of the socket facilitate hafting to a handle. In Europe the palstave was developed during the Middle Bronze Age.

posthole a hole dug in the ground which at one time held the base of an upright post. Even after the post itself has disappeared, the posthole is detectable through differences between the sediment that has replaced it and the surrounding soil.

quern a large grindstone. The early form was the saddle quern, which had a concave surface on which corn was ground by means of a smaller stone moved by hand over its surface.

radiocarbon dating a dating technique for organic, carbon-bearing substances, based on the uniform rate of decay of the carbon 14 isotope.

rights of common legal rights, held by individuals, to use specified areas of common land for purposes such as grazing and gathering plants and other materials.

ring-ditch a circular ditch that often surrounded Bronze Age barrows or funerary mounds.

totem a representation of an animal or other natural object, used as an emblem of an individual, a family or a larger social group.

tranchet axe a type of stone axe used during the Mesolithic period whose sharpness was produced and maintained by striking a sharp blow at right angles to the line of the cutting-edge.

INDEX